Work-Life Matters

David Pendleton • Peter Derbyshire
Chloe Hodgkinson

Work-Life Matters

Crafting a New Balance at Work and at Home

David Pendleton
Henley Business School
Henley Centre for Leadership
Oxfordshire, UK

Peter Derbyshire
Butleigh, UK

Chloe Hodgkinson
Edgecumbe Consulting Group Ltd
Bristol, UK

ISBN 978-3-030-77767-8   ISBN 978-3-030-77768-5 (eBook)
https://doi.org/10.1007/978-3-030-77768-5

© The Editor(s) (if applicable) and The Author(s), under exclusive licence to Springer Nature Switzerland AG 2021

This work is subject to copyright. All rights are solely and exclusively licensed by the Publisher, whether the whole or part of the material is concerned, specifically the rights of translation, reprinting, reuse of illustrations, recitation, broadcasting, reproduction on microfilms or in any other physical way, and transmission or information storage and retrieval, electronic adaptation, computer software, or by similar or dissimilar methodology now known or hereafter developed.

The use of general descriptive names, registered names, trademarks, service marks, etc. in this publication does not imply, even in the absence of a specific statement, that such names are exempt from the relevant protective laws and regulations and therefore free for general use.

The publisher, the authors and the editors are safe to assume that the advice and information in this book are believed to be true and accurate at the date of publication. Neither the publisher nor the authors or the editors give a warranty, expressed or implied, with respect to the material contained herein or for any errors or omissions that may have been made. The publisher remains neutral with regard to jurisdictional claims in published maps and institutional affiliations.

This Palgrave Macmillan imprint is published by the registered company Springer Nature Switzerland AG.
The registered company address is: Gewerbestrasse 11, 6330 Cham, Switzerland

This book is dedicated to those colleagues, family, clients and friends who have made work and home joyful.

Foreword

I was fortunate to meet David Pendleton at a pivotal point in my career, just before I stepped into the so-called C Suite (as CFO). His thoughts, knowledge and insight on leadership, motivation and relationships and why they matter were exceptionally helpful to me as my career progressed, including being the CEO of two very different companies.

Like most people, I have spent a great deal of time at work, and happily for me, I mostly enjoyed it, but was largely incapable of explaining why. This book, written by David Pendleton, Peter Derbyshire and Chloe Hodgkinson, helps unpick what it is that makes work enjoyable and addresses the challenge of how to balance work and home life: or maybe more correctly, how to get the most out of work and home life. They have managed to translate their deep academic insight into an enjoyable, thoughtful and useful read (probably an essential one in a Coronavirus ravaged world).

It sets out clear, easy to understand concepts that will help all readers discover what gives them energy, what really motivates them, what they truly enjoy and equally importantly, what sucks the life out of them and makes life miserable. It suggests different approaches to attaining increased satisfaction and reduced anxiety, and who would not want that? Whatever your preferred balance, work and home life matter and this book will help you get the best out of both. Put differently, if you are wondering whether you are working to live or living to work, this book will ensure that your focus is on what makes your life worth living.

Newbury, UK   John Rishton

John Rishton is Chair of Serco and Chair of Informa. He is also non-executive director of Unilever and Associated British Ports. Formerly, he was CEO of Rolls Royce, CEO of Royal Ahold BV and CFO of British Airways.

Acknowledgements

Knowing whom to acknowledge is far from straightforward. So many people have stimulated, inspired, commented and contributed. Friends and colleagues have always been generous with their time, enthusiasm, insight and feedback, and if precedent allowed, the three authors would gratefully thank one another!

David wishes to acknowledge his colleagues at Henley Business School. Prof. Andrew Godley has encouraged, Karis Burton has enthused and both he and Claire Hewitt have found ways to incorporate these ideas into their programmes. Professors Bernd Vogel, Claire Collins and Karen Jansen have both supported and challenged. Steve Ludlow helped both at Oxford and at Henley. Sabehia Mohammed has role modelled professionalism and organisation. David also wishes to express his gratitude and love for his musician friends and colleagues: Ruth Hammond, Valère Speranza, Charlie Stratford, Gary Alesbrook and Pete Josef. They have shown how work and play can fuse into one so that work-life balance becomes a non-sense. Their ability to submerge ego to create outstanding teamwork and bring out the best in all of us is exemplary. They are all skilful, smart and kind. Valère, also a software engineer, created a programme to analyse the data that comes from several of the exercises in this book. Finally, David wishes to thank his wife Dr Jenny King, who is unstintingly generous with her time and feedback.

Peter wishes to recognise and give thanks for the innumerable high-quality conversations with family, friends, clients and colleagues that have taken place over many years. In his stumbling attempts to help others, they have surely helped him far more. The focus of these conversations has always been to get to a better truth. In particular, conversations with Margaret Heffernan stand out. She has a mind that sees through the veil of confusion and prejudice which often obscures our collective vision. One of my oldest friends, Paul Pudlo, deserves a special mention. If ever there was a seeker after truth, it is him. There are many other sources of inspiration including Viktor Frankl, Ludwig Wittgenstein and Carl Jung, as well as those diamonds of Indian literature, the Upanishads and the Bhagavad Gita.

Chloe wishes to thank past and present colleagues at Edgecumbe Consulting Group for their limitless encouragement and friendship. Special thanks go to Jon Cowell, Sarah Williams, Patrick Kelly and Bhavna Sawnani for their enthusiastic involvement in the development of several concepts and exercises contained in this book. Chloe is also deeply grateful for the support and guidance given by her family throughout the writing process, especially her parents Tracey and David, and her partner Matthew.

Finally, we are all grateful to two colleagues, both of whom are skilled and experienced in HR and development, who have taken the time to read and comment on the entire manuscript. Alan Cook, friend and former colleague, went out of his way to encourage us, providing helpful suggestions as did Susan Thornton, Assistant Director of HR from Reading University. Thanks to them both.

Contents

1 **Introduction: A Sideways Look at Work-Life Balance**   1
    Reference   5

2 **A Brief History of Work-Life Balance**   7
    2.1   Power and Authority   8
    2.2   Philanthropy   10
    2.3   Politics   12
    2.4   Power Shift and New Expectations   14
    2.5   The Machine Metaphor   17
    2.6   Summary and Conclusion   18

3 **Work Matters**   21
    3.1   Work and Mental Health   21
    3.2   Meaning and Identity   23
    3.3   Pressure and Stress   26
    3.4   Salutogenesis   29
    3.5   Employer Perspective   31
    3.6   How Different Generations Think   34
    3.7   Summary and Conclusion   36
    References   37

4	**Life Stages and Transitions**		39
	4.1	The Seasons Change	40
	4.2	The Seasons of a Man's Life	42
		4.2.1 The Novice Phase: Early Adult Transition	43
		4.2.2 Age Thirty Transition	45
		4.2.3 Mid-life Transition: Settling Down	45
	4.3	Passages and Transitions	47
	4.4	Developmental Tasks	51
	4.5	S-Curves	51
	4.6	Life Transitions and Work	52
	4.7	Summary and Conclusion	54
	References		54
5	**The Future of Work**		57
	5.1	The Work	58
	5.2	The Workforce	62
	5.3	The Workplace	64
	5.4	Forces and Scenarios	65
		5.4.1 The TIDES of Change: Five Forces of Disruption Shaping the World (This Section by Dean van Leeuwen of Tomorrow Today Consulting)	66
		5.4.2 Scenarios	71
	5.5	Summary and Conclusion	73
	References		74
6	**New Balance; Work-Life Balance Is Non-sense**		75
	6.1	Unhelpful Scenarios	76
	6.2	Buzz/Drain	78
	6.3	What's the Difference Between Work and a Hobby?	80
	6.4	Seeking Balance in Our Life at Work	83
	6.5	Career Choice and Daily Choice	85
	6.6	Summary and Conclusion	87

7	**Analysing Worklife**		89
	7.1	Elements of Our Worklife	89
	7.2	Exercise	95
	7.3	A Worked Example	98
	7.4	Reactive or Proactive?	100
	7.5	Summary and Conclusion	103
	Reference		103

8	**Job Crafting**		105
	8.1	The Evolution of Job Design; from Top-Down to Bottom-Up	106
	8.2	The Rise of Employeeship and Job Crafting	107
	8.3	Job Crafting in Practice	109
	8.4	Task Crafting	111
	8.5	Relational Crafting	113
	8.6	Cognitive Crafting	115
	8.7	Why Should You Care About Job Crafting?	116
	8.8	How and When Could Job Crafting Help Me?	118
		8.8.1 To Take Control of Your Well-Being	118
		8.8.2 To Support Your Development Throughout Your Career	119
		8.8.3 To Ease the Transition into Retirement	119
	8.9	But Wait, I Can't Job Craft!	120
	8.10	Practical Considerations	122
	8.11	Summary and Conclusion	123
	References		123

9	**Leadership in the Fourth Industrial Age**		125
	9.1	Leadership	128
		9.1.1 The Territory of Leadership: What Do Leaders Have to Do?	130
		9.1.2 The Leadership Tasks	131
	9.2	Summary and Conclusion	140
	References		141

10	**Enabling Job Crafting, a Call to Action**		143
	10.1 Making Job Crafting More Likely		144
	10.1.1 The Power of Perception		144
	10.1.2 Creating Opportunities		145
	10.2 Creating Opportunities Throughout the Organisation		147
	10.2.1 The Leadership Team		148
	10.2.2 Human Resources		149
	10.3 Occupational Health		152
	10.4 Line Managers		153
	10.4.1 Role Modelling		153
	10.4.2 Crafting Conversations		154
	10.4.3 Crafting Experiments		157
	10.4.4 The IKEA Effect		160
	10.5 Working with Teams		161
	10.5.1 Workloads and Repetition		162
	10.6 Summary and Conclusion		163
	References		163
11	**Balance at Home**		165
	11.1 Why We Should Craft the Home Domain		166
	11.1.1 Personal Development		167
	11.1.2 Managing Resources and Demands at Home and at Work		168
	11.2 Using Job Crafting Outside of Work		169
	11.3 Summary and Conclusion		174
Appendix: A Re-design Exercise			175
Index			183

List of Figures

Fig. 6.1	Home work buzz drain	79
Fig. 6.2	The four scenarios	80
Fig. 8.1	Job crafting Google searches. (*Interest over time: Numbers represent search interest relative to the highest point on the chart for the given region and time. A value of 100 is the peak popularity for the term. A value of 50 means that the term is half as popular. A score of 0 means there was not enough data for this term*)	109
Fig. 9.1	Leadership through time	129
Fig. 10.1	Mapping buzzes and drains	156
Fig. A1	Mapping the buzzes and drains	177
Fig. A2	Mapping the buzzes, drains and possibilities	178

List of Tables

Table 2.1	From domination to partnership	19
Table 5.1	Citrix's scenarios	72
Table 7.1	Elements of each job	90
Table 7.2	Ella's job elements	92
Table 7.3	Gavin's job elements	93
Table 7.4	Carol's job elements	98
Table 7.5	Steve's job elements now	101
Table 7.6	Steve's job elements ideally	102
Table 10.1	Amy Edmondson's safety survey (Edmondson, 2018)	146
Table A1	Examples	176
Table A2	This is what I am going to do	181

1

Introduction: A Sideways Look at Work-Life Balance

It is a poignant observation that nobody on their deathbed ever said, 'I wish I'd spent more time at work'. At the end of our lives, we tend to look back over our time with a more acute sense of perspective. Our ambitions seem less important, our worries less significant and our family, friends and relationships typically assume greater significance. Work takes a smaller role at the end of our lives than it did as they were unfolding. Yet it would be a grave error to assume that, therefore, work is relatively unimportant.

We spend at least a third of our time at work. For some the proportion is far greater. If we discount the time we spend asleep, then work looms larger: around 50% of our waking hours. In our adult lives, we give the best hours of each day and the best years of our life to our employers. Some have jobs, others have vocations, still others have a sense of their life's work or their career. For many of us, our work is a source of more than mere income. It absorbs us, frustrates us, satisfies us, defines us. Early in most conversations we ask, 'what do you do?' and bureaucracies typically ask us to specify our occupation or profession. Work matters.

The history of work and of employment is complex and tied up with national cultures, economics and the inevitable shifts that occur in social values. It is confounded by matters of dominance and subservience, prosperity and poverty, freedom and servitude. In the twentieth century, the rise of individualism further impinged on the world of work and paralleled a legal shift towards the rights of employees and away from exploitative employment in the OECD countries and others. It should come as no surprise that, in the twentieth century, there also arose the clamour for work-life balance.

Work-life balance was the initial spur for this book to be written. The motive seemed reasonable but the logic flawed. The desire to find a more balanced existence than that experienced when work dominates was understandable enough. Balancing work with life seemed nonsensical and seemed worth exploring further. The juxtaposition was curious as if life were something separate from work, which of course it is not. One is entirely contained within the other.

There were other issues that prompted us to write. The rapid advance of technology through the turn of the millennium was both exciting and frightening. It carried the possibility that work could be transformed for the better as repetitive, messy or dangerous tasks could be automated, freeing up workers' time to do more fulfilling tasks. It also carried the threat that increasing numbers of workers could be replaced, robbing millions of their livelihoods. The significance of work as a means to an end has seldom been underestimated but, in a prosperous country where provision is made for the unemployed, the fear of unemployment suggested something far greater in significance. This matter also seemed to be worth exploring.

In addition, there have been two recent recessions. The first was prompted by the financial crisis of 2008. The second was a consequence of the coronavirus pandemic of 2020. Each was bad enough but the combined effects of both were huge. Additionally, the pandemic itself caused those businesses that could still function to reconsider how and where the work was done. Enforced change accelerated the trend towards remote working and virtual organisations that had started before the pandemic. The legacy is that the pattern of work going forward is not simply a reversion to the *status quo ante*. It is up for discussion and further experimentation.

1 Introduction: A Sideways Look at Work-Life Balance

Frequently, good ideas for radical change are held back by powerful bonds that have been fashioned over time and hold the *status quo* in place. When external forces break these bonds, significant change becomes much more possible. We are in such times now. It thus behoves all of us to think about how we want to create the new world of work in the new setting in which we find ourselves. This book is directed towards that end. It is principally directed towards the workplace but touches on issues in the home at the end.

The first part of the book, Chaps. 2, 3, 4 and 5, is structured according to this unfolding story. Chapter 2 places the origins of work-life balance in a broader historical context. It considers the changing nature of employment and the emergence of a more emancipated workforce. Chapter 3 shows how and why work matters as a part of a healthy and fulfilling life. Chapter 4 examines the stages and transitions through which adult life passes and explores two emergent themes: the growth of the 'self' and the implications for the perception of work and the changing needs to which it responds. Chapter 5 is focused on the future of work. Acknowledging that the future is unpredictable, it looks at the forces that are shaping the future of work in order to glean where those forces may be leading.

The second part of the book, Chaps. 6, 7 and 8, presents a different way of thinking about the matter of balance. Chapter 6 is pivotal. It builds on the idea that work-life balance is wrongly conceived and suggests that, even if the substitution is made between life and home and the matter in hand is, therefore, *work-home balance*, there is a missing element in the analysis. The missing element is energy. In order to analyse the balance required for a healthy existence, we need to recognise that there are activities that deplete our energy or drain it and others that replenish it, that give us a buzz. The implications are considerable, but the most powerful is that we need to create balance at work *and* balance at home rather than imagine that the answer to the drain of hard work is to be found elsewhere. Chapter 7 demonstrates how the foregoing ideas and tools can be deployed to analyse our work and to reveal possible changes that would make it more appealing and self-sustaining to the benefit of employee and employer alike. Chapter 8 focuses on job crafting: an employee-led technique for fitting jobs to people rather than vice versa.

The third part of the book, Chaps. 9 and 10, switches to the matter of leadership. In Chap. 9, we argue that leadership in the fourth industrial age, as described by the Primary Colours Approach to Leadership (Pendleton et al., 2021), fits neatly both with the shifting expectations of a twenty-first-century workforce and with the changes emerging from new technology, job crafting and the post-pandemic employment landscape. Chapter 10 is a call to action and eminently practical. It suggests specific actions to be taken by senior leaders, line managers, Occupational Health, HR and development professionals to make the recommended changes happen. It focuses on 'how?'

The final part of the book is Chap. 11, which focuses on the home setting. It demonstrates that the same techniques we are recommending to analyse and make changes in our work can also be used at home. Balance is to be found in both settings: work and home. This chapter is also focused on being practical, avoiding any notion of what *should* be done. If the complete life involves some element of balance, and we believe it does, then this has to be found in each setting in which we spend significant amounts of time, hence at work *and* at home.

While we believe the ideas here are relevant for all employees and professionals, we acknowledge that it is most likely that senior leaders, line managers and HR professionals are best placed to implement them in most settings. Academics and consultants may also find the book helpful. But it would give us huge satisfaction if the techniques we have described could be accessible to all employees who want to invest a little time in shaping their work from their own perspective.

David Pendleton,[1] Peter Derbyshire[2] and Chloe Hodgkinson[3]
January 2021

---

[1] Dr David Pendleton is Professor in Leadership, Henley Business School, UK, and a member of the Henley Centre for Leadership.
[2] Peter Derbyshire is Advisor to Purely Probate, a specialist UK law practice.
[3] Chloe Hodgkinson is a Business Psychologist at Edgecumbe Consulting Group, UK.

Reference

Pendleton, D., Furnham, A., & Cowell, J. (2021). *Leadership: No more heroes* (3rd ed.). Palgrave Macmillan.

2

A Brief History of Work-Life Balance

It is tempting to believe that all current preoccupations have contemporary origins. This is not quite true of the current concern with work-life balance. The dichotomy between work and leisure can be traced back to the nineteenth century and the specific issue of work-life balance to the early and middle twentieth century. The Jarrow March of 1936 popularised a cry with work-life balance at its heart but without mentioning the term. They chanted:

8 hours work, 8 hours play, 8 hours rest and 8 bob a day

The demand was for a balance between work, leisure, rest and fair pay (though it is now hard to imagine that 8 bob or 8 shillings a day, which is 40p/50c in today's currency, was fair pay). These demands came in stark contrast to the exploitative regimes of the nineteenth century in which 10, 12 or even more hours a day were worked by manual labourers and for six days a week. Yet, in the history of work through the millennia, the notion of work-life balance is a curiously modern one. So far as we can tell, the expression first appeared in the UK sometime in the 1970s and in the USA in the mid-1980s.

As an idea, it has roots in the shifting relationship between those in authority and those under that authority. It had political and social ramifications. It has since become a political and legislative issue which reflects changes in society, including the expectations of workers, especially parents, about what is and isn't acceptable in their lives. The fact that it has such a presence in today's world says a great deal about the shift in power that has taken place in the last 150 years from employers to employees. This shift has been brought about initially by struggle and then increasing affluence leading to choice. Struggle is typified by the strikes and marches of organised labour acting in concert. Affluence has also led to worker choice, especially for those with skills in greatest demand who have been able to negotiate more favourable terms. At the level of society, these and other changes have been embodied in legislation enshrining the rights of employees, capturing and enhancing a shift in attitudes and expectations.

In this chapter, we will plot the course of change from employer domination to employer-employee partnership and the consequences for all. We will argue that a line of increasing worker empowerment can be drawn from slavery to the current legal embodiment of employment rights, at least in the OECD countries and much of the industrialised world. The demand for a greater balance between time spent at work and elsewhere is a manifestation of this shift.

2.1 Power and Authority

The ultimate expression of power over workers was slavery, especially after war in the ancient world. The classic solution to the problem of what to do with the conquered was to enslave them and use them to enhance the lives and prosperity of the conquering nation. To do so involved taking away their capacity for determining their own lives and taking away their rights. Slaves were no longer people but chattels to be used in any way the master decided as demonstrated in the empires of Greece, Rome, Egypt and more. Life quality and duration depended on how well the slave met the slave master's needs. Slaves as workers had no rights though it is possible that smarter slave owners figured out how much more productive were those who were stronger and better fed. Yet when the supply of slaves was plentiful, it is likely that even such basic considerations were easily discarded.

As horrifying as this seems, we do well to remember that slavery in the US and Europe was only officially ended in the middle of the nineteenth century. As recently as 1829 in the USA, North Carolina Chief Justice Thomas Ruffin ruled in the State v. Mann: *The power of the master must be absolute to render the submission of the slave perfect.*

The American civil war was fought, in part, to end slavery, and 'victory' was declared in 1865, but it could be argued that the real end of slavery in the USA only happened a full century later when, in 1965, Lyndon B. Johnson managed to get the Voting Rights Act passed ensuring universal suffrage.

After the times had passed in which power was absolute, and slavery eventually gave way to employment, the situation was still highly authoritarian and working conditions were tough. The Industrial Revolution began in the 1760s in the UK, and by 1860, the county of Lancashire boasted 2560 cotton mills employing over 400,000 workers. Working conditions were hard and the working days were long, lasting between 12 and 14 hours. The working environment was unhealthy and unsafe. Weavers often suffered from tuberculosis and passed it on to others. Those who worked in a mill card room were susceptible to byssinosis, a lung disease caused by exposure to cotton dust.

Workers were not protected from dangerous parts of the machinery, and the mortality rate among the workforce, including children, was high. Children were valued because they could gain access to the insides of factory machinery that adult workers could not reach. Schooling tended to be cut short. Children were expected to help bolster the family income. Pay was poor, sometimes in the form of coupons which could be spent only at the factory shop; fines and beatings were commonplace; and no compensation was given for injury- or work-related health problems. Children were often beaten for falling asleep. In 1841 the average life expectancy of a working-class person was 45 years.

2.2 Philanthropy

Conditions for workers only started to be addressed in the legislation of the nineteenth century, almost a hundred years after the first days of the industrial revolution. By the standards of today the early industrialised state was a crude business, under-resourced, beset by poverty, ignorance and disease. This was also a time in which a fundamental shift was taking place from farm to factory: from an agrarian to an industrial and urban society. Drawing the population from the countryside to the new towns formed around the cotton mills, coal mines, steelworks and railways, the shape of society was changing. Such a major shift in the composition of society might be expected to prompt a rethink of many attitudes and practices, and so it proved. A series of Factory Acts from 1819 to 1874 gradually improved the lot of the worker, particularly children, with restrictions placed on what jobs children could do and the length of the working week, which by 1874 was limited to a mere 56 hours!

A sense of inequality, an awareness of the social ills or a fear of revolution prompted wealthy individuals to put back into society what they saw was missing or in desperately short supply. Philanthropy can be traced through the actions of wealthy merchants during the Renaissance and the wealthy financiers of Georgian England but enlightened employment rose to significance through the actions of the industrialists of the late nineteenth and early twentieth centuries such as Americans like John D Rockefeller and Andrew Carnegie, and Joseph Rowntree in the UK. These men preached a gospel of social responsibility which encouraged the wealthy to use their wealth for the benefit of society, including their duties to their workers, who were to be treated with dignity, kindness and respect. It was argued that, with power came responsibility.

Andrew Carnegie (1835–1919) was born in Dunfermline, Scotland, and the Carnegie family took passage to America when Andrew was 13. His father was a home-based weaver like many in the town, but the rise of industrialisation in Scotland made the home weaver's life in Scotland economically unviable. Settling in Pennsylvania and living in two rooms, his father took over a weaving business which unfortunately failed, putting additional financial pressure on the family. Andrew was largely self-taught from this point on. He was a voracious reader and brought in a wage to the family home from a succession of lowly tasks. But he had extraordinary drive and determination, and these jobs gradually took Andrew through a variety of business sectors where investment opportunities arose.

By the age of 30, as the Civil War ended, he had interests in steamers, iron, railroads and oil. Ten years later, in 1875, he opened his first steel plant in Pennsylvania, and by 1892 the Carnegie Steel Company was sold to JP Morgan for the equivalent of around $13 billion today. Andrew Carnegie, at 57 years, was the richest man in the world. Although Carnegie's philanthropic career began around 1870, it came to dominate his approach to business and wealth. He married at the late age of 52 and intended to distribute the majority of his wealth in his own lifetime as evidenced by his pre-nuptial agreement. His new wife agreed with his philanthropic intentions. [For more background on Andrew Carnegie see Carnegie.org—the founder's story]

The year 1889 saw the publication of Carnegie's 'Gospel of Wealth' in which he made clear his views on the obligations of the wealthy to distribute that wealth for the good of the community. He considered the hoarding of wealth unacceptable: *'Surplus wealth is a sacred trust which its possessor is bound to administer in his lifetime for the good of the community'*. He also claimed that *'the man who dies rich dies disgraced'*.

Typically, philanthropists would act when economic, health or governmental changes caused significant hardship to large sections of the population. One such British philanthropist was the Victorian Quaker Joseph Rowntree (1836–1925). Rowntree used his wealth in part to provide housing for his workers in the village of New Earswick near York and to engage in social reform. Rowntree believed that decent quality housing should be affordable by the working man and his values and practices survived him so that, by 1954, the housing stock at New Earswick had risen to 500 homes.

His interest in social research leading to social reform continued throughout his life. Although not initially a teetotaller, Rowntree made the connection between poverty and heavy drinking. He set up a number of charitable trusts to continue the work of social research and to support charitable, religious and social initiatives. Being a political realist, one of the trusts was formed as a limited company, allowing social and political work including the ownership of newspapers and the promotion of Liberalism. [For more background on Joseph Rowntree, see rowntreesociety.org.uk]

John Davison Rockefeller (1839–1937) rose from humble beginnings to become the wealthiest man in the USA. The founder of Standard Oil, and with a near monopoly in the oil business, at one time his personal fortune amounted to around 2% of the USA national economy. Yet he began his philanthropic career early when, at the age of 16 and working as an assistant bookkeeper, he gave 6% of his income to charity. He died at 97 years having spent the last 40 years of his life at his home in Westchester County, New York, where he devoted himself to targeted philanthropy in the fields of education, medicine and scientific research. He used the majority of his fortune to create foundations through which his funds could be distributed to worthwhile projects. He especially targeted wide involvement in the educational institutions he supported since he had already worked out that those with a stake in a school would go out of their way to make it successful.

Rockefeller, Carnegie, Rowntree and others had argued that, with wealth comes responsibility as well as the opportunity to distribute wealth to benefit others. Their generosity accelerated a shift in thinking, values and attitudes towards working people who had rights and needs that should be regarded as legitimate. They empowered the powerless though still within a framework of kindly authority which begat generosity rather than a fundamental redistribution of wealth and power that changed society and enabled choice of employment. In the twenty-first century, Bill Gates, Warren Buffet and others have picked up the philanthropic torch again but now to address the world's issues: a truly global vision.

2.3 Politics

Perhaps a more fundamental shift began in the field of politics and voting rights. Before 1832, voting rights in British elections were limited to men over 21, provided they owned property over a certain value; the argument being that such people paid their taxes and demonstrated having a 'stake' in the country's future. Unsurprisingly, the Government of the day was dominated by aristocratic landlords. The young, the poor and all women were simply disenfranchised. The disenfranchised had no say in national policies and no right to seek change through the ballot box.

The 1832 Reform Act gave the vote to more men but did not address regional inequalities. At that time, the south of England could elect more members of parliament than the rapidly expanding industrial towns of the north of England. By the mid-1860s less than 5% of the population had the vote. Disraeli's Conservative government forced through the Parliamentary Reform Act of 1867, which gave the vote to skilled working-class men and brought the electorate as a whole up to 2.5 million, but still only 8% of the total population. The extra votes were given to those who rented rather than owned property. The 1884 version of the Act gave the same voting rights to rural shire counties as boroughs and towns and so increased the electorate to 18% of the population. It was not until the Representation of the People Act of 1918, reflecting the need for some positive action at the end of the truly devastating First World War, that votes were extended to all men over 21 and women over 30 years of age.

Some rights had been given; others contested. Women's struggle for democratic equality with men had its own dramatic journey. Formed in 1872, the National Society for Women's Suffrage provided a nationwide platform for women's rights to vote and so share in the nation's decision-making. Progress was slow and members' patience limited. The Government was unresponsive. Gradually the movement became more militant as the Society morphed into the Women's Social and Political Union of 1903 led by Emmeline Pankhurst.

Pankhurst had been involved in the suffragist movement since 1880. The growing militancy attracted disfavour from the (male) political elite. Pankhurst and other members of the movement were arrested and imprisoned for increasing levels of protest such as attacks on property and the rush on Parliament of October 1908. Imprisonment was met with hunger strikes. In June 1913 Emily Wilding Davison threw herself in front of the King's horse 'Amner', which was running in the Derby. Davison died of her injuries four days later. History is divided on whether this action or the generally disruptive activities of the suffragettes hastened or delayed the emancipation of women. With the Representation of the People Act 1918, the suffragettes' work was done, women now had the vote and the movement was disbanded, despite the age difference in the voting rights of men and women.

2.4 Power Shift and New Expectations

The periods 1914–1918 and 1939–1945 saw the world embroiled in two great conflicts where most endeavour and much of the national wealth went into the war effort. In the USA, defence spending spiked at 41% of GDP during Second World War. British defence spending rose to 46% of GDP in 1943. The Second World War saw 77 million allied combatants and 29 million axis combatants. Inevitably, social reform and public sector spending takes second place when the nation is involved in such a 'total war'.

When the war ended, however, the British public turned their attentions back to social reform. To the surprise of many, in the first post-Second World War general election, the British voting public took the dramatic step of ousting from power that great saviour of the nation, Winston Churchill. Churchill had defined himself as the war leader and formed a successful coalition with the Labour Party to run the government during five long years of war. Once peace was achieved the coalition was disbanded, but public opinion had not gone into hibernation during the war years simply because there was a war to win. Churchill was expected to be a shoo-in at the 1946 general election because of his success in the war but the Tories had failed to notice the tide of public opinion moving strongly in favour of the Labour opposition, who won a huge majority of 183 seats at the 1946 election.

The Labour movement spoke for the common man, promising a fairer society having embraced the Beveridge Report of 1942. William Beveridge was a Liberal social reformer who identified the 'Giant Evils' besetting Britain at the time namely want, squalor, idleness, disease and poverty. The Report, despite the country being completely absorbed in war, changed the political landscape fundamentally to one of social reform including social security payments, a national health service and employment reforms. Churchill and the Conservative party as a whole did not grasp the significance of the report and the swing in public opinion. The Tories were also accused of putting obstacles in the way of reform without suggesting credible alternatives. So, against all expectations, Churchill was dumped by a clear majority as the country voted for change and what quickly became known as the Welfare State.

It is surprising that such a forward-thinking report should come at this time. The picture during the winter of 1942 showed a global war far from being decided. The German army was bogged down at Stalingrad and Rommel's Africa Corps were being pushed back in North Africa. America had gone on the offensive against Japan following the Pearl Harbour attack a year earlier, but by winter 1942 American forces were still fighting the Japanese at Guadalcanal. The invasion of Europe was still 18 months away. What today we call the Welfare State was born at a time of great hardship, struggle and loss. It may be that the Beveridge Report[1] had more poignancy, more clout, because it came at such a time, giving the electorate a sense of a fairer society once the war had been won. By adopting the Report, the Labour Party had given the nation a compelling picture of a better future. Even a world war could not halt a social tide that was turning.

Other developments in society were starting to exert influence on decision-makers and the writing was on the wall for the age of forced compliance. The trade union movement grew out of the early industrial revolution with the principle of collective bargaining as a means of improving the lot of all members. It is clear the factory owners would not have been motivated to do so without the pressure of a workforce beginning to understand its own power of resistance and negotiation.

It is likely that the trade union movement was an essential element in the history of work-life balance since it ended the era of passive acceptance of the authority of employers. Typified by the Jarrow march of 1936, the militancy of the trade union movement was blamed for blighting the British economy in the 1970s. In 1970 alone, ten million working days were lost through strike action and this time saw a rapid rise in the power of the local shop steward.

---

[1] [To hear Sir William Beveridge introduce his report, see bbc.co.uk/archive/nhs/5139.shtml].

Government and union tension came to a head in 1974 with the coal miners' union action. This caused the Ted Heath Conservative government in the UK to introduce a three-day working week lasting over two months to conserve electricity. Characterised by militancy on the part of the trade unions and legislation curtailing the power of unions by the establishment, there was at this period of British history a tug-of-war between government, boss and worker; between the requirement to keep the country running, the demands of shareholders for dividends and the demands for higher wages and better conditions by the workforce, channelled through the union; between capital and labour. These dynamic tensions represented polarised choices over where to place emphasis or invest resources. Such choices and tensions are typical of any era: the specific choices vary but tensions remain and choices have to be made. In the 1970s, it was government, boss and worker; now the polarisation seems to be between technology and automation versus the search for employment bringing a sense of meaning and purpose, though the possibilities for integration seem greater in the current context (see Chap. 5).

In the UK, the era of compliance came to a spectacular and public end in the miners' strike of 1984–1985 over pit closures and the likely end of the industry in the UK. The writing was on the wall for the UK coal industry well before 1984 as alternative types of power became available along with cheap, imported coal. The workforce had shrunk from 700,000 to 300,000 between 1957 and 1970. The miners rightly claimed they were fighting for their jobs, their industry and their communities. During the period of the strike, over 11,000 were arrested and over 8000 charged with offences.

The then Conservative government of Margaret Thatcher displayed absolute determination to break the power of the unions. The tactics had begun before the miners' strike of 1984. Flying pickets were banned as were attempts to blockade factories, public buildings or ports. The closed shop which forced individuals to join the union if they wanted a job was outlawed. These measures, plus the destitution of many mining communities and the eventual failure of the miners' leadership to persuade the membership to continue, led to a climb down and the end of the strike. This represented the greatest defeat for the trade union movement since the General Strike of 1926. The national coal industry limped on until

1992 when the remaining pits which had not already been closed were sold into private ownership. The unions had been right that the writing had been on the wall for their industry but were powerless to stop it. Despite the defeat of the unions, something fundamental had changed forever in the relationship between labour and employers.

With the benefit of hindsight, the trade union movement can be seen to have had the interests of their members at heart and a fairer society in their sights. Thirty plus years after this defining moment for successive British governments and for the trade union movement, it is difficult to establish clearly whether the trade union movement in general, and its militant period in particular, caused or merely symbolised the change in conditions for the average worker we see today but it is more likely that they helped more than hindered. It is clear, however, that these periods and events continued a shift in power away from employer domination through worker militancy to a new relationship in which each had to take more seriously the needs and desires of the other.

2.5 The Machine Metaphor

As the power shift between workers and employers was taking place for political and economic reasons, there persisted a legacy from the industrial revolution that reinforced a dehumanising approach to organisations and labour. Organisations can be thought of as machines in which employees are mere components. Recruitment, in this context, is simply sourcing and obtaining higher quality components. Though employees are people, they become, in this scheme, human resources that sit alongside other resources such as a strong balance sheet and the possession of intellectual property. Induction is a means of running the components in, much as an internal combustion engine had to be run-in in order to function well and last a long time. In return for the loss of autonomy, time away from the family and not being treated as an individual, reward is given and dubbed 'compensation'.

The machine metaphor is powerful and pervasive. When the machine ceases to be efficient, it needs to be fixed. If it is too costly to run, components can be removed. If it could run more efficiently elsewhere, the whole machine can be relocated. If the compensation is too expensive, it needs to be reduced so that more can be done with less.

None of this implies that employment is bad. It is rather that language and metaphor have a formative effect. What begins as a convenient way of thinking about an organisation enters the language and begins to shape behaviour. In the same way, Winston Churchill is said to have commented on Parliament: first we create our institutions, then they create us. So, first we create our metaphors, then they create us, shaping our attitudes and behaviour, though whether the attitudes came first is reminiscent of chickens and eggs.

The machine metaphor has been persistent. It has been not so much an era as a vector: a force that has restrained thinking about organisations and hindered its evolution to a more humane approach. Yet, the machine metaphor is breaking down as our society has begun to think of organisations as communities of practitioners, families or partnerships. These more organic metaphors enable new ways to organise and imply new relationships between investors and labour which may entail employment, bosses and subordinates or which may transcend such hierarchical notions entirely.

Indeed, the emerging organisations in the twenty-first century may not be formally structured and incorporated at all but rather temporary, virtual or symbiotic. Whereas, legal structures, capital and ownership defined organisations in the past, the organisations of today and tomorrow may be defined much more by purpose, values and shared activities and thus, when the purpose or values change, so might the organisation to give way to new expressions of the old purpose and new organisations that temporarily embrace the new purpose while it lasts.

2.6   Summary and Conclusion

The story so far has passed through several clear stages from domination to a more egalitarian sharing of power between employer and employee. These stages can be described and summarised as follows in Table 2.1:

The early days of slavery and domination moved through to a time of employer philanthropy and worker gratitude for kindness. There

Table 2.1 From domination to partnership

Era	Domination	Patronage	Militancy	Engagement	Partnership and purpose
Characterised by	Slavery and coercion	Authoritarian philanthropy	Workers' rights enshrined in law	Shared decision-making	Employee choice

Compiled by the authors

followed a period of continuing but diminishing compliance with authority in the early twentieth century. As the twentieth century progressed, there arose militancy which jolted the employer-employee relationship into a new realism. As the twentieth century gave way to the twenty-first century, there emerged a new era of shared power and ultimately of genuine employee choice which is the ultimate granter of power in a new relationship with new expectations on both sides. Despite the two major recessions caused by the financial crisis of 2008 and then the coronavirus pandemic of 2020, shared power and employee choice still characterise the new organisations that have survived.

The key to this latest shift is purpose: the joint pursuit of clearly defined and worthwhile aims that inspire all stakeholders from owners to employees and which the customers understand and support. Allied to purpose is values: the guidelines that indicate how the shared purpose is to be pursued. As purpose and values move more to the centre stage, the engagement of the whole person becomes real. At that point, a desire for work-life balance is becoming a demand and even a new norm since the whole person has a life outside of work to which he or she is as committed as to the purpose pursued at work.

Over the course of the chapters that follow, we show that this new era, this new norm, has implications for individual employees, teams and organisations alike. Next, we will explore why work matters to specific individuals; the benefits and risks they face, and what organisations can do to maintain a positively charged work environment. We look at the power of meaning in the lives of people and how well-being is affected where meaning is lost.

3

Work Matters

In this chapter we look at the impact of work on people. Work matters and is an important part of people's lives but we may only realise how important work is when we lose it. Those who live at or near the breadline need a means of feeding themselves and their families. Work provides an income that can mean the difference between life and death. Yet the majority of people in employment work for more complex reasons and those who lose their jobs do not only lose an income but something much more fundamental: they lose a sense of identity and self-worth. In later chapters, we will consider how aspects of the working experience can enhance the lives and motivation of those doing the work or can drain energy, motivation, self-esteem and ultimately the capacity to do the job in hand. In this chapter, however, we are concerned with more fundamental matters.

3.1 Work and Mental Health

If you can fill the unforgiving minute, With sixty seconds' worth of distance run, Yours is the Earth and everything that's in it. (Rudyard Kipling—If, 1910)

Kipling's famous poem speaks of the relationship between effort and what is of value to human beings. While many of us bemoan aspects of our working lives, the time spent commuting, the nature of the task, the size of the pay packet, those we have to work alongside and so on, the act of working at all can bring many benefits.

So important is work considered to be that in 1948 the United Nations adopted and proclaimed the Universal Declaration of Human Rights, including Article 23, which states:

Everyone has the right to work, to free choice of employment, to just and favourable conditions of work and to protection against unemployment.

But why should work, as a generality, need to be enshrined as a human right? Roughly contemporaneously, Albert Camus had offered a compatible thought that is often quoted but of uncertain derivation: '*Without work, all life goes rotten. But when work is soulless, life stifles and dies*'. Evidence suggests this is right. The Royal College of Psychiatrists in an article titled *Is Work Good for You?* lists the ways work provides for us beyond earning a living. The list includes social contacts and support; structured use of our time; the opportunity to develop skills, social status and a sense of identity; and personal achievement.[1] On the flip side, the unemployed are likely to be less active and have more health problems. In later Chaps. 7, 8 and 10 we will consider the antidote to work becoming soulless.

There is clear evidence that periods of unemployment have a deleterious impact on emotional well-being. For example, one European study (Backhans & Hemmingsson, 2012) found that extended periods of unemployment led to significant levels of mental distress and that this was worse for men than for women. It was also worse for those who were used to working overtime and whose previous employment was strong in social support.

One of the biggest and most powerful studies in recent years, however, was a meta-analysis of 237 cross-sectional studies and 87 longitudinal studies by Karsten Paul and Klaus Moser in 2009. It confirmed that

---

[1] http://www.rcpsych.ac.uk/usefulresources/workandmentalhealth/worker/isworkgoodforyou.aspx

unemployed people showed more distress than those who were employed but its findings were able to go further due to the power of the analysis, which was made possible by the huge, aggregated sample size. It showed differences in distress, depression, anxiety, psychosomatic symptoms, subjective well-being and self-esteem. It also showed that the average number of people with psychological problems among the unemployed was 34%, more than twice the proportion among the employed.

The study confirmed that unemployed men were more distressed than unemployed women and also showed that people with blue-collar jobs were more distressed by unemployment than people with white-collar jobs. These effects were made worse the longer the unemployment continued, especially in countries where income distribution was poor and where there was little unemployment protection. On a more optimistic note, the study found that intervention programmes for unemployed people were moderately effective in ameliorating unemployment-related distress among those who were continuously unemployed.

These studies demonstrate the effect of lost income compounded with a greater sense of personal loss: of social support, identity and even self-esteem. In the case of loss there is an almost inevitable grief in response. Unsurprisingly, there is an increased risk of suicide among the unemployed. Work matters on many different levels. With unemployment, the sense of loss is deep and its impact powerful.

3.2 Meaning and Identity

Work is one way in which we find meaning in our lives and is closely related to our sense of identity. Although not wishing to get too wrapped up in definitions, 'meaning' here is used as shorthand for what gives the individual purpose and motivation. Identity is closely related. Although in most Western countries we do not go through the informative bowing ritual characteristic of Japan, when strangers meet, a very early question is 'What do you do?' and the answer is significant to both parties. It is one way in which we form opinions of each other and, often inaccurately, form lasting impressions of the status, values and behaviour of the new companion. We may, on that basis, decide to continue the conversation or move on, to form a relationship or not, to feel uncomfortable or relaxed. A great deal follows from such an early, simple question about employment.

There is no easy way of dealing with the lack of gainful employment in such conversations. Unemployed professionals often resort to saying who they are rather than what they do. They find it easier to say 'I am an accountant' rather than what they do with their time. To answer strictly might require them to say, 'I walk the dog', or 'not much', or even 'I look for work'. Recently retired people are in a similar bind, though it is easier to say 'I am now retired' than 'I am unemployed' since there is less stigma attached. Yet there are some similar effects of retirement to those found in unemployment with a rise in distress and a period of adjustment required from the world of work. Anecdotally, it seems that few people at work care much about what people used to do or used to be. Retired friends have pointed out the brief uneasy silence that has to be overcome in such social encounters.

Yet it is not just the reactions of others that give rise to distress. It is also a personal matter and this is where meaning is key. The Swiss psychologist Carl Jung famously said, 'Man cannot stand a meaningless life'. Put starkly, Jung is saying that without a sense of meaning the individual will not thrive. Another famous psychiatrist and neurologist, the Austrian Viktor Frankl, endured and survived three years' internment by the Nazis firstly in Theresienstadt in Czechoslovakia then in Auschwitz concentration camps, and subsequently wrote *Man's Search for Meaning*. On a daily basis Frankl witnessed fellow inmates of the concentration camp lose meaning in their lives, deteriorate physically and in spirit, give up hope and die. We can find a similar theme in the Bible, 'Where there is no vision, the people perish' (Proverbs 29:18).

As humans we find meaning in many places: in our personal relationships and family lives, through our hobbies and other pastimes, through learning and education (formal and informal), in our individual or collective endeavours, and of course in our work. Meaning seems to derive from those aspects of our life that show our connection with something greater than ourselves. 'Meaning' in this sense is a curiously undefined term; we are most aware of it when meaning is lacking in our lives. When we have a sense that our life is generally going well, it is unlikely we will stop to consider what gives our life meaning.

At other times when life is not so good, we begin to focus on what is missing, on what we perceive as a gap in our lives. At times like these, individuals may respond according to personality; some will blame others for their plight and get angry with whoever is in their sights while others retreat into a shell and may react with thoughts, feelings and behaviours associated with depression, anxiety and other forms of distress. Such conditions, familiar to most of us at some point in our lives, are characterised by absence: an absence of fun, of energy, of motivation or even of purpose. Work can bring meaning to life because it provides focus, motivation and results in return for our time, energy and commitment. Work matters because it can provide many 'invisible' benefits like a sense of purpose and self-esteem and so bolsters our mental health.

These factors came into particular focus during the lockdowns required by the Coronavirus pandemic of 2020. At this time, work for many people was separated from the location in which it was conducted. Factories, shops and offices were closed for many who were asked to work from home. For others, furlough (temporarily suspended employment) mitigated the risk of redundancy. Still others lost their jobs as some businesses discovered they could not survive despite the various grants, loans and other arrangements made by the government.

For a while, morale held up surprisingly well but, as the lockdown dragged on and the initial enthusiasm for videoconferencing waned or morphed into irritation, deeper factors emerged. Three were especially widespread. First, colleagues missed the banter and contact with colleagues that the workplace facilitated. They recognised that, with casual, spontaneous contacts came camaraderie, motivation, morale and even sparks of creativity. Second, many people experienced a loss of routine that marks out our days, months and years. Weekends were, for many, indistinguishable from weekdays and working days from holidays, though with nowhere to go. Third, people experienced an increase in fatigue caused by the greater intensity of videoconferenced conversations compared with face-to-face.

There were some upsides, however, and interviews, surveys and articles spoke of the new possibilities that enforced change seemed to be opening up. Many of the new working practices were welcomed and were likely to be sustained in any new emerging normality. And it is likely that any stigma attached to working from home, work being suspended or even redundancy was reduced due to the ubiquity of these matters. The commonplace was unremarkable, though still the loss of employment brought serious stress and despondency to add to any grief caused by deeper loss of loved ones.

Neuroscience sheds some light on this. Hilary Scarlett in her 2016 book 'Neuroscience for organisational change' points out that the conditions under which our brains thrive are defined by Self-esteem, Purpose, Autonomy, Certainty, Equity and Social Relations. She coined the acronym SPACES as a mnemonic. For most of us, work provides a sense of purpose, self-esteem and social relations. For many at work there is also an opportunity for a measure of autonomy, a degree of certainty and a sense of fairness or equity. The absence of work takes a great deal of these factors away in whole or in part. It seems that there are sound anatomical and physiological processes that reinforce and underpin the idea that work matters though the picture is not simple since massive and rapid change in many walks of life puts several of these factors under strain or removes them completely.

3.3 Pressure and Stress

We have seen that work can bring economic, health, social and psychological benefits. Yet work is not without its costs. Pressure is a fact of life and an increasingly powerful feature of our experience of work.

We have known for more than 100 years that pressure can aid performance up to a point (Yerkes and Dodson 1908). Performance suffers if there is insufficient physiological arousal and pressure stimulates arousal. However, when arousal rises to higher levels, we start to feel stressed and performance again suffers. The relationship between pressure (arousal) and performance is described as an inverted U-curve. Yet the point of maximum performance cannot be sustained in the longer term because it feels uncomfortable and chronic pressure leads to chronic fatigue and, ultimately, collapse. Thus, to sustain a high level of optimum performance means living with a degree of pressure and learning how to manage its consequences and it is possible to build up some degree of tolerance to pressure over time.

So we can become caught in a conundrum. We need pressure to perform well and strong performance is both satisfying and rewarding. Yet attempts to maximise performance put us at risk of collapse. We want to perform well and reap associated rewards, tangible or intangible, but we do not want to put our health at risk. A Marxist analysis of work suggests that work for which we have to be 'compensated' is inherently alienating. By contrast, a thought that has variously been attributed to a broad range of people from Confucius to Tony Bennett suggests that we can so enjoy our job that we never have to work again. This is the point at which, presumably, work *becomes* play rather than having to be relieved by it. In any event, most of us seek balance of some kind, like the Jarrow marchers seeking work, rest and play, to sustain ourselves in the longer term.

High levels of arousal can be prompted by a broad range of experiences: positive as well as negative. But the labelling of an experience as positive or negative is a matter of personal perspective. To some extent, we can choose whether an experience is regarded as positive or negative. A trip on a rollercoaster is stressful to some, exciting to others. Tackling new tasks, playing a high stakes game, taking on a difficult challenge could all be positive or negative according to our perception of it. In the words of Shakespeare's Hamlet to Rosencrantz, 'there is nothing either good or bad but thinking makes it so'. Indeed, a range of helping interventions from coaching to cognitive behaviour therapy are founded on this principle.

Individuals differ in these respects. Some are sensation seeking, typically extraverts, others sensation averse, more typically introverts. Some love the buzz when adrenalin flows, others hate it. These are differences in personality. Yet there is also a matter of choice. We can adopt a negative attitude to an experience or take a more positive view by an act of sheer will. For most of us, many of these individual differences are relatively stable by the time we reach adulthood, though by no means fixed. We know what we find stressful and what we find satisfying: what gives us energy or depletes it. Access to doing those things that are satisfying is deeply rewarding and having to do things we personally find stressful is typically punitive. In this respect, common experience of reinforcing our preferences in this way stands in contrast to the neurological findings on the brain's flexibility and ability to change generally referred to as *neuroplasticity*. The balance between opportunities to maximise reward and minimise distress is a telling dimension along which jobs differ for all.

So what is it that makes one context enjoyable, even thrilling, and another debilitating and stressful? What is stress? A 2007 report from the Work Foundation entitled *Stress at Work* declares stress to be elusive to define but profoundly significant in its impact: 'it is a personal experience caused by pressure or demands on an individual and impacts upon the individual's ability to cope or rather, his/her perception of that ability'. The Health & Safety Executive's (HSE) own definition is 'The adverse reaction people have to excessive pressures or other types of demand placed on them at work'. So stress, like pressure, is an internal reaction to a set of external circumstances. On the one hand, pressure may result in greater job and personal satisfaction if we meet it positively and the pressure is containable, part of what Maslow called 'self-actualisation': building confidence, self-esteem and a general sense of making progress. Stress, on the other hand, creates a sense of not having control of one's environment and the potential positives of pressure flip over into the negatives of stress; excitement becomes fear, the sense of being in control is lost and autonomy is diminished.

A lot is now known about the physiological, emotional and mental impacts of stress. At the physical level, higher blood pressure can occur in the short term and, in the longer term, heart disease, loss of appetite, poor muscle tone, osteoporosis and immune system suppression. Emotionally, the stressed person may experience changing moods, a disturbed sleep pattern and negative thoughts and depression. Related research has shown that stressful jobs can be as bad for health as smoking and obesity and that stress increases the likelihood of obesity, smoking and drinking (see the 1998 WHO report *Social determinants of health* by RG Wilkinson).

These are all the potential costs associated with a busy job. We thrive on some aspects of the work, want the income, identify ourselves with our work roles or professions. We can turn a blind eye to the stressful elements for a while but we know that these tend to catch up with us eventually. It is as if we are addicted and helpless to overcome the addiction. We want the highs, the buzz, but we do not want to pay the price that is probably inevitable.

3.4 Salutogenesis

So pervasive has been the tension between the positive and negative aspects of work that it has become the source of theory and research in its own right. In 1979, Aaron Antonovsky proposed salutogenesis (the study of the origins of health and well-being) as the complementary study to pathogenesis (the study of the origins of disease). Earlier, at the start of the twentieth century, Kurt Lewin (1920) had pointed out the two-faced nature of work: 'a means for living or a purpose in life; something demanding or equally fulfilling' (Jenny et al., 2017), a theme picked up and expanded by Schallberger (2006) who noted that 'the role of work in wellbeing and health can be understood only when we describe work simultaneously as a possible source of negative (e.g. work stress) and positive (e.g. pleasure in work) emotional states'.

Antonovsky (1987) distinguished clearly between those factors at work that eliminated stressors as distinct from other factors that seemed to be health enhancing. He also proposed that each of these factors had an impact on what he called 'sense of coherence'. Health seems to be associated with a greater sense of coherence, ill-health with its reduction or disturbance. Workplaces that enhance this sense of coherence are characterised by meaningfulness, manageability and comprehensibility, and this relationship has been taken up by many other researchers (see Jenny et al., 2017 for a thorough and helpful guide to this topic and associated research). This body of research purports to have identified the positive health-enhancing and performance-enhancing effects of activities that promote a greater sense of coherence at work.

Antonovsky (1987) specifically emphasised consistency, workload balance and opportunities to participate in decision-making as positive factors in building up the sense of coherence of employees. Generically, he was asserting that the nature of the working environment could enhance or deplete the strength of the sense of coherence. And these assertions have been supported by research studies in a variety of contexts leading Jenny et al. (2017) to conclude that 'sense of coherence (a) is influenced by various aspects of work and organisation, (b) influences work-related outcomes such as burnout and stress symptoms and (c) moderates the effects of unfavourable conditions on health outcomes'.

At the heart of this research is the idea that there is a clear relationship between demands, control and support. Two researchers, Karasek and Theorell, created in 1990 a demand-control-support model and proposed two hypotheses to test. The first was that jobs with high mental job demands and low control or social support lead to mental strain and illness among workers. The second was that jobs with high mental demands where control and support were also high lead to increased learning, motivation and a feeling of mastery which inhibit the potentially harmful effects of work-related strain. Jenny et al. (2017) report that the first hypothesis has been confirmed in several studies but that the second hypothesis and the proposed mitigating effect of learning and mastery have seldom been investigated. But, they report, several studies have demonstrated a mitigating effect of high employee engagement on the experience of depression at work.

In further developments of these ideas, the relationship between *job demands and resources* has been investigated and a JD-R model proposed. *Demands* require sustained physical or psychological effort whereas *resources* help achieve goals, reduce demands or stimulate personal growth and development. Hence there are both positive, motivational processes and negative, health-impairing processes (Schaufeli & Taris, 2014; Bakker & Demerouti, 2007). In other words, Jenny et al. (2017) point out, both pathogenic and salutogenic pathways are in evidence.

The key implication in this research is that the factors in the work and in the workplace that enhance the sense of coherence of employees, and the associated gains in health, well-being and productivity, can be created by deliberate effort. If an employer wants to help to create such a workplace, it can be done (Becker et al., 2010). If an employee wishes to enhance his or her sense of coherence, this can also be done by reflection and reconnecting with a sense of vocation and meaning in the work: a process described as 'self-tuning' by Vinje and Mittelmark (2006). To this end, Vogt and colleagues in 2013 published a work-related sense of coherence (Work-SoC) scale. Comprising just nine questions, the robust and validated Work-SoC scale examines the perceived comprehensibility, manageability and meaningfulness of an individual's current work situation (Vogt et al., 2013; Bauer et al., 2015). Crucially, however, self-tuning and the search for meaning may be hard if the enterprise in which one is working is not well-regarded.

3.5 Employer Perspective

While work-related stress clearly impacts the individual, the organisation also pays the price. A survey by the UK's Health and Safety Executive (HSE) in 2014/2015 concluded that lost working days due to anxiety and stress in the UK totalled 9.9 million days, or 35% of all days lost through ill-health, representing a total cost of about £6.5 Bn. The European Agency for Safety and Health at Work published similarly costly findings in their 2014 literature review and report 'Calculating the cost of work-related stress and psychosocial risks'. The Stevenson Farmer review (Deloitte 2017) published a figure of £33–42 billion as the cost to employers of poor mental health in the UK in general. The UK also has a well-documented problem with chronically low productivity and this likely to be one consequence of diminished performance brought about by excessive pressure and stress. In 2015, the TUC stated that 'every two minutes, a worker somewhere in the UK is made ill through stress at work'.

In the US, it is often cited that the economy loses about $300 billion in sick leave, long-term disability and excessive job turnover (Rosch, 2001) although this figure is often disputed as a gross over-guestimate. Nevertheless, claims for stress-related disability are the fastest-growing category in the US and Europe.

Viewed from broad occupational categories, professional groups experienced more stress than other workers. In both men and women, the age ranges 45–54 reported the highest levels of work-related stress with women reporting overall higher levels than men. The HSE report also pointed out that public service jobs (education, social services, health and defence) showed higher levels of stress than other jobs. The HSE report listed seven potential causes of work-related stress: demands, (lack of) control, poor relationships, frequent change, role complexity, (lack of) support and cultural issues. Culture they defined as 'how it [the organisation] approaches and manages work-related stress when it arises'. Of course, many of these stress-creating factors can become wrapped up in matters of management and leadership since managers have a powerful effect on workload, autonomy, change, role complexity, support and culture (see CIPD 2016). It is also likely that dealing with stress *when it arises* means frequently dealing with a crisis rather than seeking ways to prevent, anticipate and avoid it in the first place.

Christina Maslach (1982), Professor of Psychology at University of California, Berkeley, carried out considerable research from the 1970s on what she came to call 'burnout' being 'a psychological syndrome of emotional exhaustion, depersonalisation, and reduced personal accomplishment'. She charts the downward spiral as emotional energy is depleted and workers feel unable to give themselves to their tasks and begin to see themselves and their efforts negatively. In such circumstances attitude to co-workers deteriorates. We become cynical, even callous, disregarding their needs and their contribution to the work effort. Rather than doing one's very best, cynicism produces the bare minimum effort to get by at work and avoid being sacked. Naturally, this produces an erosion of efficacy and, by not feeling good about oneself at work, self-esteem deteriorates and self-motivation disappears. This situation has consequences for the individual, their co-workers and the organisation for which they work. To quantify this, the UK Working Lives survey (2018) estimated that while 30% of workers feel full of energy at work, 25% rarely or never feel this way and 10% regularly feel miserable when at work. What is more, middle managers seem to feel this pressure more than other groups.

The impact on the organisation is no less dramatic than for teams or individuals bringing poor quality of work, low productivity, low morale, absenteeism, staff turnover, health problems and depression. Such a cocktail of negative emotion and behaviour is bound to spill over into family life causing problems there. Respondents to the research often spoke of not sleeping, not enjoying spare time or family life; professionals described losing that critical sense of dispassionate objectivity with clients or patients.

Individuals facing unremitting work overload are likely to feel they have lost a measure of autonomy, and the more this becomes widespread, the more the work community becomes dysfunctional. A heightened sense of injustice follows, and resentful attention becomes paid to relatively small examples of unfairness: who gets to work on the 'best' projects, who gets a window with a nicer view, who gets the parking spaces closest to the reception area and the like.

So how can any of this change? Maslach argues that in any shared social context, such as work, co-workers have a reciprocal influence on each other. Co-workers can create stress by being rude or uncivil, bullying or abusive or engaging in negative conflict. Rhona Flin (2010) showed that even witnessing rudeness might impair memory and creativity. Similarly, co-workers can provide help and support, mutual trust and even friendship. The best medicine for burnout is a major shift in the social context. Potentially, burnout might be turned into work engagement, exhaustion into energy, cynicism into involvement. She also emphasises that effort should be put into creating a positive work environment rather than dealing with the negative. This kind of positive environment would comprise a sustainable workload, rebuilding the individual's sense of control, giving recognition and appropriate reward, creating a supportive work community, demonstrating fairness, mutual respect and social justice. In related research, Christine Porath reported in the Harvard Business Review of 2014 a study of 20,000 employees around the globe, that those who get respect from their leaders report greater health and well-being, more trust and safety, greater enjoyment and satisfaction with their jobs, greater focus and prioritisation and much more meaning and significance in their work.

Incidentally, we should note that these are all changes that can be made in the workplace and do not imply less time at work, nor, incidentally, do they imply any great financial outlay to achieve. Certainly, these issues concern what happens in the workplace rather than the time we spend away from it.

3.6 How Different Generations Think

Stress-related matters are always likely to have been important to get right but especially now that there are different cohorts of people coming through the workforce. The Advisory, Conciliation and Arbitration Service (ACAS) report of 2012 looked into the views and expectations of young people entering employment and the corresponding views of their employers. It found that, while employers were generally clear about what skills they wanted their new employees to have, they were less clear in devising appropriate strategies for easing young adults into their first job. There was little earlier research about the perceptions and thoughts of those young adults taking this important first step into the world of work, or of their early experience of working life. The ACAS research found young people were intimidated and anxious facing what they considered to be unrealistic expectations from employers.

As well as the new entrants to the world of work, at any point in time up to four generations of workers can be found in many organisations. The generations currently in question are those born between 1946 and 1964, 'Baby Boomers', those born between 1965 and 1985 'Generation Xers' and those born after 1985 'Generation Ys or Millennials'. Those born after 1999 are dubbed Generation Z. Though the precise start and finish dates of each generation's birth is somewhat approximate, the key to this categorisation is the differing values of each generation leading to different attitudes to work and differing degrees of compliance with authority as explored in Chap. 2.

Whilst there are major differences between individuals in all these groups, there are also thought, controversially, to be characteristic differences between the groups. 'Baby Boomers' are thought to distrust authority a little, are more open to change but also bring into the workplace more of a sense of personal entitlement. They are prepared to work hard and are generally optimistic about their lives. Retirement, now approaching for this group, is seen more as a career transition into other activity rather than a cessation of activity.

'Generation Xers' naturally seem to question authority and more than preceding generations are very interested in the concept of work-life balance. 'Xers' are very adaptive and willing to accept challenges. They are independent thinkers, self-reliant and entrepreneurial. Xers can be very protective of family time.

'Millennials' are the first global generation born into the internet age and have always known the threat of global terrorism. Entrepreneurial, many will have had jobs before leaving school. They have never known a world without mobile devices and see themselves as global citizens, eager to travel. As we write, we have just passed the tipping point in which Millennials are now more than 50% of the workforce and most organisations comprise around 75% Xers and Millennials.

According to some, different generations come to work with somewhat different values and perspectives. To generalise (wildly): 'Boomers' seem to value hard work and being a team player; 'Xers' value life balance and diversity; and Millennials value diversity and making a difference in the world. It is the employer's job to mould these differing views into efficient and effective organisations and teams. There are also contextual factors to consider as the workplace changes: changes in job security, average length of tenure in a job, the possibility of one or more career changes, the rise of the portfolio career, the emergence of entirely new jobs and categories of jobs as technology advances and society changes.

Employers early in the twentieth century may have been able to get away with treating their people with a casual disregard to their needs and even those who employed largely baby boomers may have been able to appeal to their loyalty and willingness to get on with the job. But Xers and Millennials are less likely to just go along with whatever the employer wants. They want more autonomy and choice. They have lives and want to live them fully, and they have high expectations of what satisfying work comprises. They want balance between work and other aspects of their lives, and they are becoming aware that there is also the possibility of balance *at* work.

The evidence on these matters, however, is controversial, and it has been pointed out that there are greater differences between personality types, irrespective of generational differences. Melissa Wong and colleagues, for example, writing in the *Journal of Managerial Psychology* in 2008, examined generational differences in personality and motivation. They concluded that there was little evidence of these generational stereotypes, encouraging managers to focus more on individual differences rather than relying on so-called generational differences. For our purposes, however, the implications are similar either way: attitudinal differences exist and need to be a part of managerial thinking if we are to bring out the best in colleagues at work.

In this context, it is not just Apple and Google who are creating games areas, cafes, creativity spaces and crèches at work but also more mainstream organisations who are responding to the broader wishes and needs of employees. The boundaries between home and work, work and leisure, toil and fun are becoming increasingly blurred and for good reasons.

3.7 Summary and Conclusion

Work matters because it literally 'puts food on the table'. Work matters because it is a significant part of our lives but our sense of work 'mattering' rests on how well we are in ourselves, physically, mentally and emotionally. Work matters because it impacts directly on our sense of well-being and life fulfilment. Work matters because it helps provide a sense of purpose and meaning to our lives as well as structure to our time. Work matters because it provides a sense of camaraderie, of belonging to a team, a unit, an organisation. Work matters because it can directly affect our health. In short: work matters.

Yet there is also a cost associated with work and the cost is frequently associated with the stresses and strains that work entails. The balance between the upside and the downside of work, its ups and downs, is a matter of increasing significance to different cohorts coming through the workplace and employers need to pay increasingly close attention to how an appropriate balance is struck. The clear implication is that energy at work can be increased or decreased by what happens in the workplace and the matter of rest and recuperation is related.

References

Antonovsky, A. (1987). *Unravelling the mystery of health: How people manage stress and stay well*. Jossey-Bass.

Backhans, M. C., & Hemmingsson, T. (2012). *European Journal of Public Health, 22*, 429–433.

Bakker, A. B., & Demerouti, E. (2007). The job demands-resources model: State of the art. *Journal of Managerial Psychology, 22*(3), 309–328.

Bauer, G. F., Vogt, K., Inauen, A., & Jenny, G. J. (2015). Work-SoC- Entwicklung und Validierung einer Skala zur Erfassung des arbeitsbezogenen Kohärenzgefühls. *Zeitschrift Für Gesundheitspsychologie, 23*(1), 20–30.

Becker, C. M., Glascoff, M. A., & Felts, W. M. (2010). Salutogenesis 30 years later: Where do we go from here? *International Electronic Journal of Health Education, 13*, 25–32.

CIPD. (2016). *Absence management survey report*. London.

Deloitte. (2017). *Mental health and employers: the case for investment. Analysis to support the Stevenson-Farmer review*. London.

Flin, R. (2010). Rudeness at work. *British Medical Journal, 340*, c2480. https://doi.org/10.1136/bmj.c2480.

Jenny, J. G., Bauer, G. F., Vinje, H. F., Vogt, K., & Torp, S. (2017). The application of salutogenesis to work. In M. B. Mittelmark, S. Sagy, M. Eriksson, G. Bauer, J. M. Pelikan, B. Lindström, & G. A. Espnes (Eds.), *The handbook of salutogenesis*. Springer International Publishing. https://doi.org/10.1007/978-3-319-04600-6_20.

Karasek, R. A., & Theorell, T. (1990). *Healthy work: Stress, productivity, and the reconstruction of working life*. Basic Books.

Karsten, I. P., & Moser, K. (2009). Unemployment impairs mental health: Meta-analyses. *Journal of Vocational Behaviour, 74*, 264–282.

Lewin, K. (1920). *Die Sozialisierung des Taylorsystems. Eine grundsätzliche Untersuchung zur Arbeits und Berufspsychologie*. Verlag für Gesellschaft und Erziehung.

Maslach, C. (1982). *Burnout: The cost of caring*. Prentice Hall.

Porath, C. (2014, November 19). Half of employees don't feel respected by their bosses. *Harvard Business Review*.

Rosch, P. J. (2001). The quandary of job stress compensation. *Health and Stress, 3*, 1–4.

Scarlett, H. (2016). *Neuroscience for organisational change*. Kogan Page.

Schallberger, U. (2006). Die zwei Gesichter der Arbeit und ihre Rolle für das Wohlbefinden: Eine aktivierungstheoretische Interpretation [The two faces of work and their roles in well-being: An interpretation based on activation theory]. *Wirtschaftspsychologie: Sonderheft Zur Salutogenese in Der Arbeit, 2*(3), 97–103.

Schaufeli, W. B., & Taris, T. W. (2014). A critical review of the Job Demands-Resources Model: Implications for improving work and health. In G. F. Bauer & O. Hämmig (Eds.), *Bridging occupational, organizational and public health* (pp. 43–68). Springer.

UK Working Lives Survey Report. (2018). CIPD. https://www.cipd.co.uk/knowledge/work/trends/uk-working-lives

Vinje, H. F., & Mittelmark, M. B. (2006). Deflecting the path to burn-out among community health nurses: How the effective practice of self-tuning renews job engagement. *International Journal of Mental Health Promotion, 8*(4), 36–47.

Vogt, K., Jenny, G. J., & Bauer, G. F. (2013). Comprehensibility, manageability and meaningfulness at work: Construct validity of a scale measuring work-related sense of coherence. *SA Journal of Industrial Psychology, 39*(1), 1–8.

Yerkes, R. M., & Dodson, J. D. (1908). The relation of strength of stimulus to rapidity of habit-formation. *Journal of Comparative Neurology and Psychology, 18*(5), 459–482. https://doi.org/10.1002/cne.920180503.

Wong, M., Gardiner, E., Lang, W., & Coulon, L. (2008). Generational differences in personality and motivation: Do they exist and what are the implications for the workplace? *Journal of Managerial Psychology, 23*(8), 878–890.

4

Life Stages and Transitions

The course of an individual life is unique, but when aggregated with the lives of many others, a predictable and well-documented pattern emerges. Instantly recognisable are the life stages of infant, child, teenager, young adult, adult, and old age. Shakespeare said in As You Like It '…one man in his time plays many parts'. From the infant 'Mewling and puking' to the schoolboy, the lover ('Sighing like a furnace'), the soldier, the judge, the 'lean and slippered pantaloon' and finally to 'second childishness and mere oblivion'. Each particular stage plays a vital part in our physical, mental and emotional growth and, eventually, gives way to the next phase, discarded like the moulted skin of a snake. Our physical process of change is mirrored by changes in attitude, emotion, values and preferences. The snake's journey to its new skin is described as often stressful and advice is available for pet owners on how to reduce its stress level. It is important to bear in mind that the movement, or *transition*, from one stage to the next can be traumatic for humans too!

This chapter looks at some of the research into the major phases of life and the place work holds in our lives while going through the different stages. Moving from one life phase to the next is a transition. Transitions bring with them a challenge to the way we see the world, as one way of seeing gives way to the next. Our reaction to each transition is critical. At each stage, there is a binary choice: to accept and go with the flow or to resist or deny that change is happening. This choice has real consequences for us. Research we will review below has shown that transitions can be tremendous developmental opportunities provided we embrace the change. Failure to embrace the change, or resistance to it, causes stagnation in the individual.

Inevitably, the place work has in our lives must also shift, subtly or dramatically, from one life phase to the next. How we see ourselves also changes over time and it is important to recognise the transient nature of this self-image and indeed what I call 'me'. The employer response to these inevitable life transitions is likely to be important for each individual and can help ease the transitions so that motivation and productivity are maintained.

4.1 The Seasons Change

The Greek philosopher Heraclitus (c.535–c.475 BC) gave the world the famous quote 'There is nothing permanent except change'. We can often think of ourselves as bodies with minds attached, yet the body itself is in a state of constant change. The human version of the snake shedding its skin goes largely unseen. At the cellular level, renewal (aka change) is happening at a phenomenal rate. On average cells in the small intestine turn over every two–four days, stomach cells every two–nine days. Even our skeletal structure is not permanent. Osteoblasts, which secrete the substance making and repairing bones, turn over every three months and stem cells every two months (see *Cell Biology by the Numbers*).

Life expectancy in the UK currently averages 79.3 years for men and 82.9 years for women. The facts are indisputable: humans age, become sick and die. Within our bodies an impressive chemical and biological industry is maintaining and renewing our cells and never takes time off even for a well-earned rest. With very few exceptions (the lens cells in the eye, the central nervous system) we have no physical continuity at the cellular level with the infant, the adolescent, the young adult, even the body a year ago.

Despite these rapid cellular changes, we maintain a belief that our body is the same one we had as a child, just bigger and stronger. Despite the lack of empirical evidence, we have no problem in maintaining this enduring sense of self because we have and sustain a psychological construct we call 'me'. Yet, looking back along the timeline of our respective lives, we can remember thinking differently, having very different tastes in foods, reacting and relating to others and situations very differently and so on. More importantly, that timeline represents growth and learning. Each time a new thought arises, a new body of knowledge is encountered, a new taste is discovered, we absorb and systematise what has been learned. If the learning is sufficiently significant, as opposed to merely gathering information, our being shifts ever so slightly on its axis and we are changed by it. This is particularly true of new knowledge which challenges the way we believe ourselves or our world to be.

For those of us involved in education, it is both rewarding and astounding to watch students absorb and codify new information and in a short time become able to wield the knowledge with authority and confidence: in short, to make it their own. Reflecting on our timeline, we can now see that, along with our bodily change, our sense of self is changing to accommodate the lifelong learning underway. Despite changing almost everything we identify with, there is still an enduring sense of self which forms the vehicle, the continuity between who we were and who we will become. This can be called *individuation*; the binding principle which, according to Jung, enables us all to form a viable personality. It begins at birth and over time, establishes the boundary between me and the world. The young infant knows no such boundary. There is no boundary between the baby self and the outer world. As we will see later, life transitions require more than just self-awareness and some courage; they also need a 'self' to grieve for the phase being abandoned and to generate the positivity to embrace the phase ahead. This is not the same as the ego principle because the ego struggles with life changes and is happier identifying with a set of life circumstances as if they were set in stone.

The challenge for us is to face the evidence that our inner and outer environment is in movement. The natural world is in constant flux. At times, this movement is dramatic: like the emergence of a pandemic or a tsunami. At other times, the movement is so slow and subtle we can ignore it, but we do so at our peril.

At one level our individual lives appear to be unique. Only I have had the complex blend of nature and nurture, of experience, of successes and setbacks, of beliefs and so on. While this is undoubtedly true, it belies the fact that we share our lives with many others. As a child, we did not sit in a solitary classroom, but we were corralled with many others. As an adult, our choice of work not only reflects personal skillset and bias, but also reflects the options available at the time and in our culture: trade, medicine, law, education, finance, craft and so on. Not only do we share a vast commonality with others in our upbringing, our culture and our type of work, but we also share *life phases* with our contemporaries.

We automatically recognise the phases of infant, child, adolescent, young adult, middle life adult, retiree and elderly. We recognise in theory the movement, the transition from one life stage or phase to the next. It is tempting to suppose these transitions are as painless as they are automatic but the experience of the transition is not always smooth. In the book of Corinthians in the Bible, chapter 13 verse 11 we read 'When I was a child, I spoke as a child, I understood as a child, I thought as a child: but when I became a man, I put away childish things'. Whether this transition, from child to adult, or from one adult phase to the next is as simple as putting away, the previous phase's 'toys' were explored by two surveys carried out during the 1970s, which found that the lived experience is more complex and demanding than simply shutting the door on the previous phase, and that some of us choose not to move between phases despite strong impulses to do so.

4.2 The Seasons of a Man's Life

In 1978 Daniel Levinson with colleagues published an important study *The Seasons of a Man's Life*. The study explored the in-depth life stories of a group of 40 men from 35 to 45 years.[1] They were taken from a variety

---

[1] The study was entirely based on men. The implications for women were not addressed, but later in the chapter we look at the work of Gail Sheehy, whose study was of both sexes.

of backgrounds, both socially and occupationally. Despite their differences the study group displayed strong correlations in their stories. From these emerged two main phases in the working life of a man called the novice phase and settling down phase.

4.2.1 The Novice Phase: Early Adult Transition

Levinson created a coherent narrative of the phases of male adult life beginning with the 'novice stage' typically lasting from years 17 to 29. The investigation showed that this first adult-proper stage carried a series of major tasks. For the novice adult, the initial task is to formulate a Dream, initially poorly articulated, of the life the individual wants as an adult. The task at this stage is to flesh out this dream. Tension is likely between significant others (e.g. parents pushing the individual towards a career) and the essence of the Dream which may well be at odds with the wishes of parents. Maintaining the Dream is important because a surrender or betrayal of the Dream will have consequences later. The second task is to form a mentor relationship which may or may not be in the workplace. 'Mentor' here suggests teacher, adviser or sponsor. The role of mentor is to facilitate the realisation of the Dream. The third task is to form an occupation. This is more complicated than simply picking a career: an extended process rather than a simple choice. Those who choose strong occupational commitment in their early twenties often come to regret it later. Some individuals may have several false starts and begin again in a different occupation. This process can last for years.

A 2019 survey published by the UK Office for National Statistics showed that young adults between 16 and 24 years have a much higher likelihood of changing jobs (up to 30%) compared with those in the age range 35–49 (10%). Those in middle years 25 to 34 have a 16% likelihood of a job switch. By the time one reaches the age of 50+, the rate drops to 5%.

The final task of this phase is the formulation of love relationships. Although likely to be accompanied by 'marker events' like weddings or childbirth, the process of forming such relationships starts well before the marker event and continues long beyond.

Another way of viewing the novice adult entering the world is to think of the task of fashioning a provisional *life structure* capable of linking what one values in oneself and the adult society one encounters. There exists a dichotomy between exploring the potential, the adventure of this period and the requirement to begin to build a stable life structure. Finding a balance between these contrary claims is not easy. Enjoying too much of the adventure can generate a rootless, transient life whereas, if the building of stability holds sway, it can amount to a denial of the Dream.

Throughout this phase there is the excitement of discovering the adult world, yet this period also raises fundamental questions of identity. The British rap artist Michael Ebenezer Kwadjo Omari Owuo Jr, also known as Stormzy, found himself on the cover of Time Magazine in 2019 under the title 'Next Generation Leaders'. Stormzy, 26 at the time, summed up the confusion of the novice phase, amplified considerably by the fame pressed on him by saying

> *I am deeply flawed and still learning how to be a man and still figuring out how to grow into the person I need to be but within all of that confusion and all the juggling of being a human and trying to be a superhuman—I have purpose. And my purpose has led me here.*

As well as individuals shifting focus, meaning and purpose during a lifetime, so generations shift in attitudes to life and work, as we pointed out in Chap. 3. In their 2016 report on the attitudes to the workplace of millennials (people reaching adulthood from 2000 onwards), Gallup found fundamental changes in attitudes towards work, bosses and colleagues. In brief, Gallup found that millennials preferred purpose to salary, personal development over job satisfaction, bosses who coach rather than control, regular communication over annual appraisals, to develop their strengths rather than fix their weaknesses, and see their work as so much more than just a job because it's their life.

4.2.2 Age Thirty Transition

At or around the age of 30 the novice life structure is found wanting and work begins on a more satisfactory life structure. The provisional nature of the twenties period is ending and life is getting more serious. Typically, the age thirty transition, starting around age 28 and lasting roughly 5 years, begins with a sense of uneasiness, that something is wrong or missing, and that something else is needed to make the future worthwhile. We are *en route* to our middle years but not quite there yet. The provisional quality of our 20s is drawing to a close, and a greater sense of urgency arises. Life becomes 'for real' and now is the time to change things for the better.

For some, the 'age thirty transition' is smooth and seamless, without disruption or crisis. Relationships are good, family life is stable and their occupation is providing rewards. The previous life structure can be built on with confidence and so enrich one's life. A different reality greets those who have a painful transition at this point in their lives. It can be a source of stress and anxiety and Levinson's study showed it to be a common phenomenon, a sense of not having the clarity about where one is headed or the ability to make the jump to middle life.

4.2.3 Mid-life Transition: Settling Down

Beginning at around 32 or 33 years, and spanning 6–9 years, we transition to our mid-life. Mid-life is characterised by certain relationships and aspirations achieving greater prominence whereas others are demoted or set aside altogether. This makes possible a stable and satisfying life ahead, by the creation of the next life structure which, and once fully adopted, will be very hard to change.

As with the novice stage, our settling down phase carries a number of major tasks. Establishing one's niche in society is pivotal. This is the period when we put down strong roots and get serious about our interests. Everything happens within a well-defined pattern. We work at building a better life for ourselves and family, improving our skills, becoming more creative and contributing more to society.

The major tasks for this phase begin with terminating the previous early adulthood era. We find ourselves reviewing and reappraising life up to this point, coupled with a heightened awareness of our own mortality. Highly charged questions can arise: What have I got to show for my life? What do I really want for me and my family? We may discover that our life to this point is somewhat illusory; that long held beliefs about oneself and the world simply do not hold. It is a difficult time, creating feelings of loss as much as joy and liberation. We must also initiate middle adulthood and begin planning the next phase. Even if we stay in the same work, changes in the character of work such as advances in technology, organisation structure or within oneself will have to be accommodated. Such inner changes may affect how much, and exactly what the individual wants to give the world.

It is also a time when inner polarities become apparent like those of destruction and creation. We all have the potential for both and will have acted out both poles at times within our work and/or home lives. The developmental task at this phase is to deeply understand the destructiveness within oneself and in the world at large. Things done to me (my grievances) must be understood along with the things I have done to others (my guilt). We have to deal with these polarities; otherwise they will cause division.

This is the time to become the hero of the early Dream. We have become a recognised member of the tribe. Early in this phase we have shed the apprentice badge to become a fully fledged adult. Later on, we achieve seniority and recognition. Naturally, there is a perceived need to maintain a stable life structure. Still the tension remains between the Dream and the world. We now have authority, can speak with our own voice and are generally less dependent on others. At least, that is the theory. The reality may not be anything like as smooth. If we can make progress during this phase within a stable structure, our efforts at advancement are likely to succeed despite the hardships. The stresses are real but manageable and the benefits outweigh them. If we experience a *failure or decline* within a reasonably stable life structure, the costs can be high. We may have lost a job or are unable to make progress beyond a certain limit having repercussions for our self-esteem and family life. The accountant who will never make partner and the hospital doctor forever stuck at the registrar grade are examples that come to mind. More seriously, we may lose the sense of meaning in our lives. There are many well-known examples of decline in which the costs are high. One that famously hit the national headlines in the 1970s was that of Simon Dee. Dee was described by the Guardian newspaper reporting his death in 2009 as a 'huge radio and television star of the swinging sixties whose career went into freefall in the 1970s'. Dee had a glamorous lifestyle and a place among the rich and famous for a time and ended destitute as a bus driver.

Despite the apparent stability of our life structure, it may not be what we want and we attempt a new life structure by *breaking out* of the constraining one. We have an urgent sense of the flaws of the life structure; a new awareness making the life currently lived intolerable. This new perspective may focus on work, marriage and even oneself, becoming profoundly alienated from one's world. This is a time of crisis. Crucial aspects of the being cannot be expressed and pressure from the world to be something else is unacceptable.

We may be *very successful*, achieving a promotion that lifts us out of the life structure. We have a new role, much higher income and tasks requiring new aspects of ourselves to come to the fore. The challenge here is to *maintain the connection* with who we are; otherwise advancement becomes a curse, projecting us into an alien world.

4.3   Passages and Transitions

Gail Sheehy's book *Passages* presents another interesting view on the potential seasons of the lifespan. It was the result of a 3-year study and 115 in-depth interviews. Although published back in 1976, there is a timelessness to the study and its conclusions because they speak to the human condition. Sheehy differentiates between an external and an internal system. The so-called external system includes our work, social class, family and social roles, and represents the way in which we present ourselves to the world. The internal system is a world where meanings are ascribed to the individual's participation in the world. The codification of experience and the application of meaning are critical parts of one's mental life and indeed one's mental health.

Carl Jung, the great psychologist and psychotherapist, said, 'Man cannot stand a meaningless life' (1959). He also described transitions as episodes of disequilibrium. The importance of meaning to the individual's inner realm or system was dramatically illustrated by Viktor Frankl's depiction of life in the extermination camps he survived during the Second World War (Frankl, 1959). Day after day he watched his fellow inmates lose some crucial connection, some essential inner meaning, and they just died.

Brilliantly caricatured by Douglas Adams (1979), the notion of a single question producing a simple answer to the meaning of our lives is plainly facile. The meaning of one's life, as a finite statement, may never be known or even graspable but we keep adding to and revising our store of meaning. The meanings we ascribe to people, work tasks, hobbies and so on are powered by an inner dynamic and a creative energy. Falling in love is one example. The object of our affection obliterates most, if not all other considerations or distractions. The burst of inner realm energy is enormous and the meaning given to 'this is the one' is overpowering.

Sheehy argues that it is the inner system that tells us it is time to move on from the current phase to the next. This impulse for change is already within the inner system; it doesn't have to be created nor can it be found anywhere else. Sheehy refers to these messages as 'crucial shifts in the bedrock' of who we think we are. By accepting and embracing these life changes, we are taking a chance exactly because we are leaving behind what was familiar and safe and moving into uncharted seas in a boat we don't yet know how to operate. Each transition leaves us exposed and vulnerable, but also 'yeasty and embryonic'. From this starting line, new possibilities arise and new energy can be found to explore them. But such vulnerability will also be uncomfortable, in part because our body of meanings making up who we think we are is under challenge.

For some, the vulnerability and uncertainty caused by transitions becomes undesirable. A delaying or obstructing element can arise which keeps us anchored to a passing life phase despite it representing a no longer relevant way of being. Some consistently refuse to recognise the inner realm and its significance, ignoring the subtle messages of the need for change. In her 2020 book, *Too Much and Never Enough*, Mary L Trump wrote of her famous uncle Donald 'NYMA [the military academy Donald

Trump attended] reinforced Donald's aversion to vulnerability, which is essential for tapping into love and creativity, because it can also expose us to shame, something he could not tolerate'.

It is tempting to correlate life transitions with major events in our lives such as leaving home, settling down, having a family, joining or leaving a chosen career path. However, of themselves such milestones do not present developmental opportunities. They can do so of course, but the real developmental work is in the inner realm, in facing the challenges these major moments present.

For Sheehy, the *passages* (or transitions) from one life phase to the next are characterised by subtle changes in perception, a shift in the sense of self in relation to others, a shift in the relative balance between safety and danger we feel, our perception of time (relaxed or running out) and a gut-level awareness of being alive versus stagnating. The signals we receive are subtle, requiring us to be alert to changes in the inner system, and to be willing to listen to the restlessness, the dissatisfaction, without reaching automatically for a quick fix solution (new partner, new car, new job, new outfit etc.)

Each transition presents both threat and opportunity. The life passages are not discrete or tidy: life is a messy business and one's inner system can certainly get messy. The unease caused by the shift, the transition, shows us that one's current life structure has run its course, and now it's time to move on.

Sheehy identifies the first adult phase as the 'Trying Twenties' where the fundamental task is to move into, and grasp hold of, the adult world. Two contrary impulses are in play. Firstly, there is the need for a firm, safe life structure in which strong commitments can be made like choice of career, residence and life partner. Secondly comes the desire to explore and experiment. If one chooses experimentation, the whole of the 20s can be a transient state. In whatever way we balance these impulses, a *life pattern* can be set in motion, for example permanently locked into safe structures and relationships, the permanently transient, the 'wunderkind' (risk-taker; always playing to win) or the caregiver. The danger of this kind of locked-in state is the likely resistance to future changes and is worsened by the avoidance of any self-examination.

Then follows the CATCH-30s, where the life created in one's 20s begins to appear narrow or restricted. This restriction manifests perhaps as outgrowing the chosen career or personal choices made in the previous decade. The common response is to tear up the 20s' life structure. Through this transition, new vitality is felt, and there is a sense of rooting (beginning to settle down) and extending (sending out new roots and shoots).

Sheehy calls the period approximating to the 35–45 years period the 'Deadline Decade' in which time shrinks. We sense the loss of youth and gradually become aware our physical powers are faltering. There may be a spiritual dimension to face: there are no absolute answers. In a time of danger and opportunity, we re-examine both our sense of purpose and the resources we have and how to spend them from now on. This moment is a major reset. There is uncertainty. We are alone. At the same time, we realise we no longer have to seek permission from others; we learn to give ourselves permission. There is also likely to be some grief for the old self we are giving up.

If we fail to read the signs, fail to listen to the inner voice and to accept and adapt, we run the risk of stagnation and resignation. We accept our lot and wait for retirement. Alternatively, if we confront this middle passage of our lives, we may find a renewed sense of purpose and a more authentic life structure through which our personal happiness improves and we can let go of limiting roles, for example hanging on to being the caregiver for children who are now independent of us.

Middle age is our time of greatest influence, where we have abandoned the wild dreams of youth and inflexible, no-longer relevant life structures. We will have experimented with techniques for facing change and accumulated practical knowledge of ourselves through which our judgement is vastly improved, enriched by both inner and outer experiences. We become sense-makers for ourselves and our lives in the same way organisational leaders are described as providing this role for colleagues and subordinates. We, and such leaders, create a credible narrative through periods of change and disruption.

4.4 Developmental Tasks

Both Levinson and Sheehy see transitions as developmental. To avoid a transition is to deny oneself essential life development. Each season/phase carries within it a developmental task. The task in early adulthood is to separate from parents and to form the adult personality. On entering the adult world, the chief task is to fashion a provisional life structure providing a workable link between the self and adult society. The task is dual and somewhat contradictory; to create stability while at the same time exploring possibilities.

In our 30s we work through the flaws noticed in the 20s' life structure. This can be a period of reform and refinement or a period of revolution. Alternatively, it can presage a crisis: the current life structure has become intolerable yet the individual is incapable of making a new one.

The mid-life transition around 45 years presents big questions like 'What have I done with my life' and 'What do I want for myself and others?' For most of the study subjects, this was a period of great struggle: a moderate to severe crisis. Levinson characterised this as the neglected parts of the self urgently seeking self-expression. External markers for this struggle could be a dramatic job change, divorce or having an affair, illness, death or relocation. Both studies show that significant shifts happen in all our lives causing us to re-evaluate who we are and what we want our lives to be.

4.5 S-Curves

Another window on the seasons of the human life cycle is the work of Peter Robertson (2005). Robertson, psychologist and management consultant, and others formulated the notion of the 'S' curve and its implications for individuals, organisations, even political structures. Originally a biological model for the life cycle of organisms, the 'S' curve describes birth (the bottom left tip of the S) followed by a difficult period for the entity establishing itself in its environment (the initial dip after the lower tip of the S), followed by a period of growth until it reaches maximum potential and output, thereafter beginning a diminution of health and vitality, eventually reaching the descending tip of the S-curve, signifying the end of the cycle and death of the organism.

Robertson found that this simple pattern played out in innumerable situations and examples. It is easy to apply the S-curve model to our physical existence, and to see ourselves travelling along our own curve. We may be at the peak of our powers or we may be well beyond that point. In *organisations*, Robertson noted that the enduring health of the organisation required insight into the effectiveness and lifespan of a particular strategy or business model; to know when the life energy of any strategy was waning; and to recognise the need to 'jump' to the next S-curve, that is the new operational strategy and begin again the cycle of expansion and growth. For example, today we are seeing the impact on the retail sector caused by society's migration to online buying. The companies that survive and thrive are likely to be those that have embraced the new approach and made the jump to the new paradigm and started on their new S-curve.

Each of the phases or seasons identified by researchers Sheehy and Levinson can be interpreted through the S-curve. Each new phase is difficult at first, as we attempt to slough off the old way of thinking and being and begin to accommodate and relate to the new. The end of each phase, signalled by those subtle messages in the inner realm, is represented by the final slope of the S-curve, urging us to jump, stagnate or die.

4.6 Life Transitions and Work

An article by Sheena E. E. Blair (2000) argued that transitions represent emotional struggles that are both conscious and unconscious which are met by a blend of thought and feeling manifesting as hope or purpose. This makes the process of transitioning an active adaptation rather than passively adjusting to a new situation. Transitioning from one life phase to the next is a complex process. As well as an inner emotional struggle of letting go of the old and taking up the new (as Levinson said, terminating the old and initiating the new), there are also interpersonal dynamics and context, both at work and at home, to consider. We are discontinuing the old and assumed pattern of life.

This can be protracted and difficult. As Blair says, 'An occupational analysis of someone experiencing this phenomenon may reveal the urge to keep active; frantically to do'. This behaviour is protective of the old life structure and its unconscious purpose seems to be to postpone acceptance of the changes necessary. There are clear links to self-image and self-esteem here, with a strong pull to stay with the old, the familiar. A leap of faith is needed to embrace the unknown in the changed situation rather than seek to retreat from it.

Blair quotes Molineux and McKay (1999) who considered the function of the occupation at points of transition. They stated that occupation is a fundamental human need and the part it plays at transition points could include a celebration of personal distinctiveness while garnering support from the experience of others; the protection of self-esteem and the sense of being able to manage the transition; and the recognition that shifts (in attitude if not in actuality) within an occupation over time are unavoidable.

How then are employers to respond to these individual life journeys? Arguably it all starts with a recognition of the existence of life stages and that the process of transitioning between stages is universal. As individuals, employers must face their own transitions, dealing with their own inner and outer struggles as the old is surrendered, preparing the groundwork for the new. So too must colleagues and subordinates experience their own transitions in turn. Employers who are sensitive to these issues can understand, anticipate and take account of these changes in individual members of staff. While the pattern is universal, each individual faces their own unique challenges. There is no 'one size fits all' here. Employers who are enabling can allow workers to adapt their work to their own emerging and changing needs. In Chaps. 6, 7 and 8 we will provide techniques to be used to do this in the context of job crafting.

4.7 Summary and Conclusion

Change is the only constant. Every life goes through recognisable phases or stages. Transitioning from one phase to the next may be straightforward but is more likely to be problematic. As the previous phase is being abandoned, we are challenged about our perceptions of ourselves, our environment and our occupation.

These life phases or stages are relatively well understood and documented. Each transition between phases offers both a potential crisis and a developmental opportunity. As individuals, we can choose to observe and learn from these challenges or we can choose to ignore them—at our peril.

We have the capacity to witness, to listen to our inner guide and to adapt to major transitions in our lives in ways that allow us to surrender what went before and to engage energetically with what lies ahead. The inner journey is mirrored by a changing external world; technology, organisational structure, economy, family and society are equally in flux.

Employers have a vital role in recognising when staff members are in transition and enabling them to modify the way they work to meet the new life phase.

References

Adams, D. (1979). *Hitchhiker's guide to the galaxy*. Pan.
Blair, S. (2000). The Centrality of Occupation during Life Transitions. *British Journal of Occupational Therapy, 63*(5), 231–237.
Cell Biology by the Numbers. http://book.bionumbers.org/how-quickly-do-different-cells-in-the-body-replace-themselves/;
Frankl, V. (1959). *Man's search for meaning*. Beacon.
Gallup. (2016). *How millennials want to work and live*. www.gallup.com/workplace/238073/millennials-work-live.aspx;
Jung, C. G. (1959). In conversation with the British interviewer, John Freeman, BBC Face To Face. https://www.youtube.com/watch?v=2AMu-G51yTY
Levinson, D. (1978). *The seasons of a man's life*. Ballantine.

Molineux, M., & McKay, E. (1999). Occupation: Reaffirming its place in our practice (Workshop). In *Inaugural United Kingdom Occupational Science Symposium: Abstracts*, College of Ripon and York St John, York.

Office for National Statistics. (ons.gov.uk); Analysis of job changers and stayers.

Office for National Statistics—Average age at death, by sex, UK dataset 2016–18.

Robertson, P. (2005). *Always change a winning team*. Marshall Cavendish Business.

Shakespeare, William. *As you like it*: Act II Scene VII.

Sheehy, G. (1976). *Passages*. Ballantine.

Trump, M. (2020). *Too much and never enough: How my family created the world's most dangerous man*. Simon and Schuster.

5

The Future of Work

The future is unknown and unknowable. Nevertheless there exist tribes of forecasters, astrologers and futurists who work to defy this general principle. They deploy a vast array of techniques from the statistical and scientific to the mystical and spiritual. And many are able to sell their wares to those who find uncertainty hard to tolerate.

The future may be unpredictable, but it is not a total mystery. It unfolds within several contexts which are eminently well known and it is shaped by forces that are reasonably well understood. The laws of physics, for example, do not change, despite the tantalising possibilities proposed by Star Trek and its siblings. We can be fairly certain, therefore, that Scotty will not be able to beam us up, at least for the foreseeable future. Warp speed is also a near-impossibility unless our understanding of the universe changes since, according to Einstein, any object accelerating to the speed of light achieves infinite mass. That probably rules out time travel also.

The future of work is a much more anodyne affair but still this chapter will not attempt to predict work's future with any degree of precision. Rather, it will consider the forces that are shaping the future of work and examine several scenarios that pose interesting questions, suggesting ways in which employers might need to prepare for *a range of possible futures* that are emerging from the mists of the present. The chapter will focus on changes affecting work itself, the workforce and the workplace as exemplified by Jeff Schwartz and colleagues (Deloitte 2019).

5.1 The Work

Advances in technology transform work. Some advances create a better mousetrap, others replace mousetraps altogether and others, it is feared, might render rodent operatives redundant. Lasers have replaced scalpels in surgery where their pin-point accuracy is highly prized, and they bring extra benefits including their ability to vaporise unwanted matter, seal small blood vessels and penetrate parts of the body that are much less accessible to conventional surgery. But the march of technology goes further. Computers controlling lasers can increasingly perform automated surgical procedures. They do not tire working through the night, their 'hands' do not shake or get cramp and they do not upset colleagues.

Automation is a major force shaping the future of work in many spheres. Pilots have joked for years that the next generation of aircraft will largely fly themselves and the cockpit will be designed for a pilot and a dog. The dog will be trained to bite the pilot if he or she touches any of the controls. The truth is not far from this. Flying an airliner is sometimes said to be 90% boredom and 10% terror but always requires a high level of vigilance. Long haul flights extend the 'boring' part: in the cruise, there is almost nothing to do and yet qualified pilots must monitor what the aircraft is doing automatically. It is argued that this is the wrong way around. Automated systems do not get bored, do not miss brief or weak signals, unlike their human counterparts. Playing humans and machines into their best roles would lead to significant changes in many aspects of work on the flight deck and elsewhere allowing the machines to fly the planes most of the time. The barrier to overcome is likely to be the reluctance of passengers to entrust their lives to an entirely automated system when they can be wrongly programmed and the faults revealed only after a catastrophe. The recent problems with the Boeing 737 Max are likely to have had a retrogressive effect on the acceptability of the automation of aircraft systems for some time.

Driverless cars pose the same challenge. They are predicted to appear on our roads in the next decade. The barriers are not technological so much as legal and financial. If a driverless car has an accident, for example, whose fault is it? Who gets sued? And who pays compensation?

Nevertheless, the balance between human beings and machines in doing work is almost certain to keep shifting towards machines as technology, automation and control systems improve. On the one hand, this balance has been shifting for generations, and, for businesses, there are very few disadvantages. Financially, there is an initial capital outlay and there are on-going maintenance, repair and replacement costs but they are typically rather small compared with the cost of labour, health and safety requirements, strikes, pensions and the like.

Morally, on the other hand, the shifting balance is something of a quagmire. For the reasons rehearsed in Chap. 3, above, work matters and workers have unsurprisingly feared, resented and opposed being displaced by machines. At the start of the industrial revolution, the spinning jenny was invented to cut the costs of labour in making yarn. In economies where labour was cheap (such as India), the spinning jenny was not deployed for many years whereas it rapidly replaced many much more expensive workers in England. The disruption created led to the replacement of workers and violent protests ensued. In the early 1800s, the term 'luddite' was coined to describe those who rioted against the advance of machines that took jobs from people. They were often thought to be opposing progress but they were not: they were opposing hunger.

The predicted replacement of workers, however, is hotly disputed by many technologists and economists. Technology can be shown to create jobs as well as replace them. Currently, the Organisation for Economic Cooperation and Development (OECD) predicts that automation could eliminate more than 14% of jobs and disrupt 32% (Nedelkoska & Quintini, 2018) while, in the same year, the World Economic Forum (WEF, 2018), in *The Future of Jobs Report*, suggested that technology could empower the workforce, creating jobs, so that a million jobs may be lost but 1.75 million could be created.

This debate has been raging for a while. Donald Fisk, in a US Department of Labor report (Fisk, 2003), described the evolving scene in the twentieth century in America. The following data are gleaned from that report:

- At the start of the twentieth century, 38% of workers in the USA worked on farms. By the end of the century, just 3% worked on farms
- At the same time, the proportion working in mining, manufacturing and construction decreased from 31% to 19%
- The proportion working in the service industries increased from 31% to 78%

Attributing the reasons for these changes, Fisk points to multifactorial influences but chief among them was technology. Significantly, however, unemployment was 5% in 1900 and roughly the same in 2000, despite the workforce increasing almost 6-fold from 24M in 1900 to 139M in 2000.

Technology and automation certainly cause change and disruption but, taken over longer timescales and looking more broadly, it is far from clear whether technology and automation destroy jobs or create them. The evidence so far seems to be that it does both and it shifts them from one place to another and from one kind to another so that a worker who is willing to retrain and adapt may be able to do so. There is an emerging concern, however, that a tipping point may have been reached in the early twenty-first century and that the wave of technological change is becoming a tsunami that will wreak havoc with jobs and employment. By contrast, there is an apparent paradox to do with productivity. As Ian Goldin and Robert Muggah put it in their excellent book *Terra Incognita* (2020):

> *If machines are substituting for, or augmenting, the jobs of workers, we should expect higher productivity. But we don't get it. On the contrary, since the turn of the millennium, we have seen a slump in productivity across the world.* (p. 166)

Carl Benedict Frey and Michael Osborne of Oxford University (Frey & Osborne, 2017), in a frequently cited research study, have estimated that fully 47% of current US jobs are highly likely to be computerised (replaced) in the next decade or two. However, they argue:

as technology races ahead, low-skill workers will reallocate to tasks that are non-susceptible to computerisation—i.e., tasks requiring creative and social intelligence. For workers to win the race… they will have to acquire creative and social skills.

Frey and Osborne also envisage that a shift will be created rather than a cataclysm. Michael Osborne envisages a positive scenario in which computers will do what they do best, allowing human beings to do what they do best. That is, that computerisation, and automation more generally, will liberate people to apply themselves to the more social and creative aspects of work they enjoy, shedding the drudge work that they do not. This is an optimistic vision of human-machine collaboration rather than a dystopian image of human-machine competition.

In support of this argument, Jeff Schwartz and colleagues (Schwartz et al., 2019) point out:

The jobs of the future are expected to be more machine-powered and data-driven than in the past but they will also likely require human skills in areas such as problem-solving, communication, listening, interpretation and design.

They too envisage a future in which machines take over repeatable tasks and the work humans do becomes much less routine: a collaborative model. However, they stress the fundamental need to create appropriate training and development so that people can learn to work in this way and so we do not find ourselves:

weighed down trying to apply legacy concepts and skills onto the new and quickly emerging world of human-machine collaboration. (p. 3)

In general, studies of the future of work regularly identify dilemmas that are provocative but unresolvable. Bernd Vogel and colleagues demonstrated this well in their collaborative survey study in 2018 entitled 'Work 2028: trends, dilemmas and choices'. The team interviewed an international sample of 50 influencers from a range of disciplines and backgrounds. They considered issues to do with organisations, work and leadership in the context of what they dubbed 'crucial trends in shifting societies'. They spelt out many dilemmas but guided their readers to implications and recommended actions, perhaps the biggest and clearest of which was that education and worker development need to equip all of us to be able to adapt: to acquire flexibility and to act.

5.2 The Workforce

Industrialisation changed the relationship between the work and the workforce. Pre-industrialisation, craftsmen produced complete products. Industrialisation broke production down into discrete tasks to automate and standardise both the processes and the products. The psychological shifts in this period must have been considerable for the craftsmen (usually men) themselves since they could no longer see the complete fruits of their labours nor take pride in the items they alone had produced. The sense of alienation must have been considerable, but the economies of industrialisation would have overwhelmed the slow and expensive production of skilled individuals. This tide of change would have been irresistible if a small reduction in the quality of an item was weighed against a significant reduction in its cost and greater standardisation. The industrial workforce comprised fewer skilled craftsmen and increasingly large proportions of unskilled workers toiling at repetitive tasks. This was the first major change in the workforce for centuries.

Other changes have happened with increasing frequency. The world wars in the twentieth century brought about another change, born of necessity. When a large proportion of working men had to leave the country to fight in the armed forces, women were brought in to factories and farms to replace them and to continue the production required. Lack of access for women to higher education meant that they tended to be confined to unskilled and low-paid work but this trend, both in education and employment, shifted through the twentieth century and increasingly well-educated women have made rapid progress into the professions and into managerial and leadership roles. There is much more progress still to be made to full equality of opportunity and parity of reward but the movement in that direction is clear.

When there is relatively full employment and widespread anti-discrimination legislation, changing demographics are reflected in the workforce. The ageing population in most Western countries is reflected in an ageing workforce. Retirement in many countries is not enforced at specific ages, and older workers are increasingly common to be found working alongside much younger colleagues. The average age of the workforce in many organisations is consequently rising.

The nature of employment is also causing a significant change in the workforce. Much is said and written about the 'gig' economy but the fuller picture encompasses much more. Whereas, in the early twentieth century, people joined companies and often were employed for life, now there is a range of employment relationships. In an organisation or on a project, employees will work alongside contractors, gig workers, employees of partner organisations, consultants and short-term casual workers, interns and apprentices. Upwork, the US freelancing specialists, estimated that 57M Americans freelanced in 2019: 35% of the workforce. This number is rising (Upwork, Freelancing in America 2019). Full-time freelancers constituted 28% of the workforce in 2019 up from 17% in 2014, and younger generations are more likely to freelance than older generations: 53% of 18–22-year olds (Gen Z) freelanced in 2019 compared to 29% of those aged 55+ (Baby Boomers).

The consequences are many and significant. Senior managers can thus build more flexible organisations, bringing in rare and expensive skills and knowledge on a temporary basis as required. Employees with skills that are in demand can experience many different projects and organisations to keep them stimulated. Engagement becomes trickier, however, and leader/managers need to find ways to co-opt team members not only into the work itself but also into the purpose, culture, vision and values of the organisation. Retention of the best is also a puzzle to be solved. All this requires that employers take engagement seriously, encouraging workers to find the meaning in their work, getting to know and understand their customers and colleagues so that they can connect the work they do with its impact on others (Schwartz, Hagel, et al., 2019 writing in the Sloan Management Review).

The challenge, in a nutshell, is to match workers' needs, aspirations, motivations and skills with the organisation's needs. This will require full involvement of the employees themselves to help craft the relationship and employment arrangements, including the nature of the work they do.

5.3 The Workplace

The industrialisation of work by breaking it into discrete tasks initially required physical proximity of the workers in a workplace where the various sub-components could be assembled into entire products. Now, both changes in work and the technologies deployed to get it done are reducing the need for proximity and hence making a traditional workplace potentially redundant. Garment factories are still common, but Zara, the Spanish clothing manufacturer and international retailer, for example has made a virtue of coordinating the efforts of individual garment makers working in their homes.

Mechanical products need to be assembled from components. Factories producing engines cast engine blocks, pistons, camshafts and the like and assemble them into whole engines and then ship them to other factories where the engines are put together with gearboxes and are assembled into body shells to produce a car. In the earliest days of motor cars, all this would have been done in one place. The atomisation of production allowed sub-components like engines to be separated from the production of the other sub-components. This trend continues and engine factories will take in smaller sub-components such as pistons or electronic components to be manufactured elsewhere and shipped to the engine assembly plants. The nature of the product and economies of scale determined the nature of the work.

Once an element of work can be separated from other elements, there is the possibility of dislocation of place. Technology also has a role to play. One of the London teaching hospitals found that they had difficulty recruiting consultant radiologists. They had to support a 24-hour service in which images had to be interpreted by highly skilled and experienced consultant physicians at all hours of the day and night to facilitate care and even save lives. So they recruited and employed radiologists in Sydney, Australia, who, by working a normal day, covered the 'night' shift in London. This was made possible by the technology that allowed images to be transmitted faithfully to Australia and the reports transmitted back again in real time. It was no longer necessary for the medical team all to be in one place whether they sat at the end of the corridor or in a location on the other side of the planet.

The broader trend is towards distributed working. Contact originally had to be physical to make work happen. Now contact can be virtual using shared platforms and systems. This makes location almost irrelevant to get a great deal of work done, especially in the service industries where physical entities are not produced but rather digital entities: data, reports, proposals, trades and images.

The telephone has facilitated distant conversations for over a hundred years but high-quality videoconferencing, once the province only of corporations or the rich, has become commonplace, reliable and convenient for all. This has been available for several years but not universally used until the coronavirus pandemic accelerated its adoption to cope with the lockdown. Now that it is ubiquitous, we complain about it and again crave the human contact afforded by the workplace. When the pandemic has passed, the new normal is likely to include a greater degree of freedom of choice about work and the workplace. As ever, the ability to choose increases quality of life and keeping pace with changing needs and preferences will require employee choice from day to day rather than once and for all. But how might we begin to think about the world to which we will have to respond or that we might want to create?

5.4 Forces and Scenarios

Since the future is unpredictable, the core issues here concern the forces that are shaping the future of work, the workforce and the workplace. Two approaches hold promise: on the one hand, identifying the forces acting on our world now to see the directions in which they are leading, and, on the other, constructing plausible alternative scenarios rather than attempting prediction. We will explore both here.

5.4.1 The TIDES of Change: Five Forces of Disruption Shaping the World (This Section by Dean van Leeuwen of Tomorrow Today Consulting)

The sceptical reader may be wondering just how much can change in a decade. We would encourage you to Google: 'New York 5th Avenue 1903'. The search will reveal a road full of horses and carts and even children playing next to a dead horse. Look closely or you will easily miss the single automobile. Now Google: 'New York 5th Avenue 1913' Images will reveal a road full of automobiles and not a single horse.

Sometimes the world changes at the snap of a finger, and a generation of children grows up in a world where they can't even imagine the world their parents and grandparents once lived in. Look at the forces of change happening in the 2020s. What will be today's children's equivalent of the 1913 automobile moment?

Will it be the end of slaughtering animals because steaks are now bio-fabricated on demand in the home using 3D food printers and Nespresso-style protein capsules? (Note from the authors: Singapore has just approved the sale of bio-manufactured chicken in December 2020). Or the proliferation of robotic chefs that learn to cook 'mamma's' secret Bolognese recipe and orders food direct from grocery retailers without you even having to lift a finger?

These possibilities may seem crazy far-fetched to us today, but a lot can change in a decade. Henry Ford's lawyer reputedly said: 'The car is a fad; the horse and cart are here to stay'. Gottlieb Daimler, the founding father of the automobile said: 'there will never be a mass market' for the sale of cars. Daimler was an enlightened leader, the inventor of a machine that vastly changed the world and yet even he failed to reimagine a world with millions of miles of paved roads, petrol stations and massive motorways. He could only see a world where there wouldn't be enough skilled chauffeurs to drive the wealthy.

History shows that breakthrough moments offer exceptional and rare opportunities to shape the future. The 2020s will be such a moment. Those leaders who are tuned to the changing forces of progress will shape the future. In a breakthrough moment there are no roadmaps—we have never been here before—What got you here will not get you there. Therefore, the great leaders during these opportune times have the mindset of explorers and a sharp desire to create rather than be shaped by the future.

Currently, our view of the world is constrained by our biases and the lenses through which we see. So, we need tools to help us to be more curious about the future of work. One such model developed by Tomorrow Today is the TIDES of Change.

TIDES is an acronym and stands for: Technology, Institutions, Demography, Environment/Ethics and Social Values. These are the five TIDES of disruptive change and using the TIDES model you can explore potential futures but let's temper expectations. TIDES is not a tool to predict the future but a tool for understanding the forces of change which we will describe briefly here.

5.4.1.1 Technology

We are living in a golden age of technology. Not since the Age of Discovery have so many pioneering spaces opened in the areas of science, health, education, engineering and even space travel. With today's emerging exponential technologies that allow so much to be done, the key question is 'what is the future we want to build together?'

Remember, it is not technology, but people who create the future. Technology is the enabler, and as Abe Lincoln said: 'The best way to predict the future, is to create it'. The true challenge leaders face today is to imagine the world not as it is, but to unlearn and reimagine the world as it could be.

We have the technology to solve the greatest problems of the world. What we need now is bold and creative leadership. With all the amazing technology from AI to self-driving cars to the ability to sequence DNA quickly and cheaply, and so on, the greatest risk of the twenty-first century is that we fall short, failing to think big enough to make this century great for everyone.

5.4.1.2 Institutional Change

Institutions are the building blocks of society; they are the structures and the bodies determining the rules of the game and how the games are played. Globally, as the Fourth Industrial Revolution begins to take root, we are seeing deep structural change at all institutional levels, and this will have a profound impact on the future of work.

There are several levels of institutions. At the highest we have geopolitical institutions. Democracy is changing. Nationalism is on the rise. The struggle for power between China and the USA is another great example, as is the disruptive impact of Brexit.

An industry is an institution. It has a 'normal', which dictates the products or services that are produced, prices charged and conduct of players. Associations ensure standards are set and adhered to, and people in the industry strive to achieve levels of accreditation indicating their ability to play by the rules of the game. But from industry to industry around the world we are seeing deep structural changes occurring as technology and other TIDES impact how the future of work is done. Think of how retail is changing. It's not just Coronavirus which is driving these changes. The shift to online buying and automation has long been visible. The pandemic is merely an amplifying force bringing home the realities of the new normal to retailers not agile enough to change or bold enough to shape their future. Many people thought Ocado's leadership had lost the plot when Waitrose dropped them as their online partner. But Ocado was resilient and stayed the course. They are now reaping the rewards of boldly believing in the trends they were seeing and their ability to shape the future of how people shop. As the adage goes, you create your own luck.

5.4.1.3 Demographic Changes

Often considered a slow-moving force there are a number of massive demographic trends which are crashing on businesses like a tsunami of change. Consider the role demography has played with the current Coronavirus crisis. It took humanity over 10,000 years for 50% of the world's population to move into cities. By 2007 around three and a half billion people now reside in urban areas. Predictions are that by 2050, 70% or seven billion people will live in cities. So, what it took 10,000 years, humans will do again but this time in just 40 years!

This level of rural-urban migration on steroids is a ticking time bomb for pandemics. If more and more people live in cramped spaces close to wet markets and trade in illegal and exotic wild animals, the risk of further pandemic outbreaks will increase. The WHO has suggested that within a decade there may be more than one pandemic for society to battle against at the same time.

People are also living longer. Predictions are that the first person to live to the age of 150 has already been born. We are living longer and will therefore have to work longer. The idea of retiring could well become an obsolete concept as people are forced to figure out ways to continue working well into their advancing ages. Especially if governments keep pushing out the retirement age, which they must or the exchequer will be bankrupt. The 100-year career may not be that far away. Demographics has the potential to be one of the greatest forces of disruption and yet most organisations pay scant attention to it.

5.4.1.4 Environment and Ethics

Earlier we mentioned that forces of disruption converge and collide during periods of great transition and nowhere can we see this better than in environment and ethics. People are questioning the ethics of business especially following the Great Recession of 2008 and the subsequent period of austerity.

Global warming and environmental destruction are leading to the rise of movements such as Extinction Rebellion. Workers, in particular millennials, prefer working for an organisation that has a purpose over and above shareholder returns. CEOs and investors are shifting their attitudes in response. At the end of 2019, the Business Roundtable, a think-tank comprising 181 of the US's largest corporates employing over 15 million employees and earning over 7 trillion dollars in annual revenue, redefined the purpose of a corporation to promote 'an economy that serves all stakeholders'. Studies by Havas, a research company, revealed that upwards of 77% of people expect companies to do more than governments to find solutions for big problems like inequality and global warming.

According to the Financial Times, assets in sustainable investment products in Europe are forecast to reach €7.6tn over the next five years, outnumbering conventional funds, as investors' growing focus on risks including climate change and social inequality pushes these strategies into the mainstream (https://www.ft.com/content/5cd6e923-81e0-4557-8cff-a02fb5e01d42). This shift will have big implications for the future of work as companies redirect capital into sustainable activities and are forced to be transparent about everything from their environmental impact to how they treat employees.

5.4.1.5 Shifting Social Values

In many ways the last of the TIDES, Social Values, is a summation of all the other disruptive forces, because if technology, institutions, demography and environment/ethics are changing, then people's values, their 'normal' or world view shifts too. Sometimes disruptions in technology are the result of shifting attitudes of people as social media technology companies like Facebook have discovered.

Other times it is a novel technology that shifts our values, for example the automobile or the smartphone. Each of the disruptive forces interacts with and influences the others. Therefore, when considering potential scenarios and various futures, it is important to explore each of the forces individually and collectively as this gives a dynamic view of potential change.

The TIDES model is not a means for predicting but rather creating the future. This can be done by asking three questions as we explore the forces:

1. What big societal problem are we trying to solve?
2. What breakthrough technology or new ways of working can be applied?
3. What is our radical idea?

5.4.2 Scenarios

Dean van Leeuwen's section above is a good example of sense-making. All good leaders, whether corporate executives, consultants or opinion-leaders, must make sense of the environment in which they are working, constructing a compelling narrative that has powerful implications for action. Dean's TIDES model is just such a compelling narrative and analysis. It offers an agenda of issues to consider with important implications for the future of work, among other matters. A fruitful alternative is to work with scenarios, though TIDES could also be the basis of plausible scenarios: a supplementary approach rather than an alternative.

The US consultancy Citrix published in 2020 a thorough scenario study about the future of work. The report, 'Work 2035', describes how they have conducted their analysis and, of course, their conclusions. The study was conducted in two stages. In the first stage, the researchers co-opted a panel of experts to help them envisage the scenarios they would then put to a wider population, in the second stage, to gauge their reactions. Their experts formed an advisory board of people they describe as 'thought-leaders from academia, think-tanks and multinational boards' who were interviewed. Keen debates were held at the end of which two critical dimensions emerged to form the framework around which their scenarios were formed. These dimensions concerned the impact of emerging technology on workers and the nature of the organisations in which, or for which, they might work.

The first distinction was whether workers are replaced or augmented (empowered/enabled) by technology. The second distinction was whether work is centralised in large organisations or distributed across smaller, agile firms and 'platform business models'. These distinctions interact to form four scenarios as in Table 5.1 (compiled by the authors from the Citrix report) thus:

The organisation then commissioned independent researchers to investigate thoroughly the opinions about these scenarios among over 1500 professionals (business leaders and employees in large and mid-market businesses) and their views of the future of work. They even added a further investigation in 2020 of the views of 300 business leaders to find out if the pandemic had changed their views. This was especially thorough.

Each scenario had its advocates and the researchers discovered some supporting evidence for each. The report sets out these various findings clearly and carefully avoids choosing a 'winner', preferring to consider the implications each scenario suggests and for which organisations and governments, *inter alia*, need to prepare. They did not discuss the possibility that these scenarios might form a sequence over time, for example, that the first to emerge could be the Powered Productives and the last to emerge might be the Platform Plug-ins.

They offered three helpful insights, however, with powerful effects, formed from those issues for which there was overwhelming support from most respondents.

- The first is that we are approaching a tipping point in which technology and AI will generate more revenue for their organisation than human workers.
- The second is that there will emerge a positive partnership between people and technology in which tech will help us work smarter, speed up decision-making and increase productivity.
- Third, that the leadership team will be a human-machine team and AI will make most business decisions.

Table 5.1 Citrix's scenarios

	Augmented worker	Replaced worker
Distributed work	Freelance Frontiers	Platform Plug-Ins
Centralised work (organisations)	Powered Productives	Automation Corporations

Helpfully for our purposes here, the report makes suggestions about how individuals and organisations can prepare for these emerging scenarios; however they work out precisely. They suggest that leaders should 'champion the human-tech partnership as a force for positive change in the workplace, bringing their employees with them'. Even more powerfully, they suggest:

> *the future that we should be planning for is one that empowers employees, making work more interesting, productive and meaningful, so that people can think, learn and create.*

This excellent study is recommended reading https://www.citrix.com/en-gb/fieldwork/employee-experience/new-ways-of-working-2035.html

5.5 Summary and Conclusion

Work is changing: the work itself, the workforce and the workplace. Technology and other factors are accelerating the pace of change and the direction of travel is broadly clear. Business models, organisations and employer-employee relationships are becoming less uniform. There is greater choice for those who are prepared and able to adapt.

Technology is having a disproportionate effect and still has the potential either to enhance or replace workers. Workers themselves tend to be fearful of its effects, concerned that their livelihoods are under threat. Yet it is just as plausible that tech will enhance their experience of work, helping create new jobs that are more engaging and bring more joy and satisfaction replacing drudgery.

The clearest implication of the analysis in this chapter is that we have an opportunity to create more positive and fulfilling work and more energising workplaces for people to think, learn and create. We are not victims of change in this respect; we are its architects and builders.

References

Citrix. (2020). *Work 2035: How people and technology will pioneer new ways of working*. Work 2035 (citrix.com)

Fisk, D. (2003). *American Labor in the 20th Century*. Washington DC: US Bureau of Labor Statistics.

Frey, C., & Osborne, M. (2017). The future of employment: How susceptible are jobs to computerisation? *Technological Forecasting & Social Change, 114*, 254–280.

Goldin, I., & Muggah, R. (2020). *Terra Incognita: 100 maps to survive the next 100 years*. Century.

Nedelkoska, L., & Quintini, G. (2018). *Automation, skills use and training*. OECD Social, Employment and Migration Working Papers, No. 202, OECD Publishing, Paris. https://doi.org/10.1787/2e2f4eea-en

Schwartz, J., Hagel, J. III, Wooll, M., & Monahan, K. (2019, February 20). Reframing the future of work. *MIT Sloane Management Review*.

Schwartz, J., Hatfield, S., Jones, R., & Anderson, S. (2019). *What is the future of work: Redefining work, workforces and workplaces*. Deloitte Insights.

Upwork. (2019). *Freelancing in America 2019*. Upwork@Global Inc..

Vogel, B., Heidelberger-Nkenke, O., Moussavian, R., Kalkanis, P., Wilckens, M., Wagner, M., & Blamke, K. (2018). *Work 2028: Trends, dilemmas and choices*. Deutsche Telekom, Detecon International and Henley Centre for Leadership/Henley Business School.

World Economic Forum. (2018). *The future of jobs report*. WEF.

6

New Balance; Work-Life Balance Is Non-sense

Since work is such an important part of life, it makes no more sense to try to balance work with life as it does to try to balance the head with the brain, the opera with the music, or the house with the kitchen. Yet 'work-life balance' is in common parlance and the proverb *all work and no play make Jack a dull boy* has been around since the seventeenth century. Of course, work-life balance is a loose formulation of the balance that is sought between work and home. But why? Why do we seek such a balance? Machines that are balanced minimise the friction and the wear and tear of operation. They run for longer without breaking down. People likewise. Recipes that are balanced are not dominated by a single flavour. Yet the balance sought between work and home seems to suggest that, without a deliberate effort to correct it, life can be dominated by work in a way that is hard to sustain and that does not feel right. There are several unhelpful scenarios that are worth exploring.

6.1 Unhelpful Scenarios

1. *The Exhausted*

There are those who find work is exhausting and they need to go home to recuperate. Work may be too busy, stressful, relentless or thankless to be tolerable. It may be that we simply don't like what we do or suffer enough negative characteristics of the work and workplace to leave us unhappy and drained. The doctor with too many patients to see, the taxi driver who must work 16 hours per day to make ends meet or the manager whose targets are beyond challenging and whose boss is never satisfied are typical. These examples conjure up images of the overworked, under-paid and under-appreciated. They are the workers who find that work drains them of their energy and they need to go home to recharge their batteries: to be ready for the next day which will be more of the same.

As common as this may be, what is happening is inappropriate. Work is proving to be such a burden that respite is required. Work that drains us and leaves us with no energy for the rest of our day is *unsustainable*. Yet increasing numbers of people are enduring this if the figures on workplace stress, cited in Chap. 3, are to be believed. And at times of rising unemployment, the race to be more effective and productive than one's peers conjures up images of those dance marathons of the 1930s where, in order to win, the couple had to be the last ones standing.

However, it is not inappropriate *because* it is unsustainable. It is inappropriate also because it is *indefensible*. It is inappropriate because it is abusive. It is a form of *theft*. The employer is effectively stealing resources from the home. In this scenario, energy is being depleted at work and replaced at home. This renewed energy is then again depleted at work and so on.

Imagine that, instead of an intangible resource such as energy, we are describing money. The equivalent would be that work is short of cash and the worker goes home, drains the family of its cash and goes to work the next day to give the money to the employer. It is just as inappropriate when the resource in question is energy, motivation, joie de vivre and the like. The principle is broadly similar if not identical. It is inappropriate to take resources from the home and give it to the employer. If the employer depends on such a transaction in order to keep the output flowing, then he or she is treating employees as assets that can be exploited. If not theft, and the family willingly gives their time to an enterprise they support, then this is charity and the donors are the family of the employee. That is not the employment contract nor, indeed, the *psychological contract* to which most people have signed up or, if made explicit, would sign up.

2. *The Frustrated*

Of course, there are those whose problem is the exact reverse. There are those who have such a miserable home life that work is a haven of tranquillity and one of the few sources of satisfaction. There are many versions:

- The parents of monosyllabic and alienated teenagers
- Those who are trapped living with their in-laws, poignantly described as 'homeless at home' in public sector affordable housing circles
- The victims of the dilapidated home that needs constant DIY to hold back the ravages of time and neglect
- The dweller in the home in multiple ownership (HMO) sharing basic amenities
- Partners in an abusive relationship

Home in these scenarios may be depressing, frustrating and apparently inescapable. These examples are far from trivial to those who are trapped in them and there are many more examples: the loveless marriage, the chronically sick family member, the anti-social neighbours or the constantly dissatisfied partner. In these scenarios, work comes as a blessed relief and an intermittent route to normality, satisfaction, self-esteem, safety and regained control. During the pandemic of 2020, this escape route was often blocked and the consequences for some were stark as domestic violence increased.

Naturally, this scenario is as unsustainable as the first. It is likely to lead to a breakdown of some kind. This may be in the form of divorce or ill-health, but the breakdown is rendered more likely as the situation passes from acute to chronic to permanent. It is unhealthy but can drag on for long periods, squeezing the joy out of life.

3. *The Depressed*

As bad as 'the exhausted' and 'the frustrated' make us feel, it could be worse: both scenarios combine for some where both work and home are out of control and miserable. There are people whose experiences of work and home are largely bad. Work is joyless and so is home. Unrealistic and relentless family demands are only matched by those of the boss at work. There is little happiness in either place and the variety in the sources of the unhappiness is far from the spice of life. There is no respite: it is a horror story. If it does not lead to suicide, it is likely to lead to depression if nothing changes. Escape may take the form of seeking a third place in which to find joy: a hobby, a club, an affair. Yet these options also raise the dreadful possibility that failure or greater disaster will be encountered in this place also. It may prove to be a salvation but could further confirm that life is just not worth living.

4. *The Delighted*

How many people at any time are likely to be in the blissful state of finding work and home are both terrific? Some will certainly be in this place and more power to them! Life will seem to be synergistic: each element reinforcing the others and creating joy on joy. Yet the moment that one of these elements starts to take a dip, pressure increases on the others to compensate and the situation risks becoming one of those described above. These times of broad delight are to be treasured but are hard to sustain for many within life's usual vicissitudes. They become like a sailboat at sea which is perfectly trimmed for the conditions, and then a squall arises that changes everything.

6.2 Buzz/Drain

Whether considering our time at work or at home, it's patently clear we enjoy some activities more than others. We can recognise the positive elements of our work or home lives, because on balance they give energy rather than deplete it. The negative elements tend to drain energy. The

6 New Balance; Work-Life Balance Is Non-sense

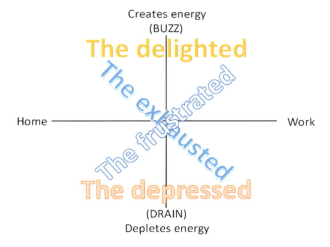

Fig. 6.1 Home work buzz drain

four scenarios above represent overall situations and can be captured in Fig. 6.1 (compiled by the authors) in which work and home form the X-axis and the Y-axis shows energy created (buzz) or depleted (drain). In physics, the law of conservation of energy states that energy can neither be created nor destroyed. But when it comes to human, psychological energy, it certainly can be as our various scenarios described.

The exhausted are shown to be living on the diagonal in which work drains them and home replenishes them. The frustrated are living on the opposite diagonal in which home drains them and work replenishes. The depressed are shown to be in negative territory at home and at work. The delighted are living the dream suggested by both work and home being in positive territory. Figure 6.2 shows the scenarios differently.[1]

These are all different ways of formulating the traditional approach to what we have come to know as work-life balance. Yet the other dimension is as relevant: perhaps what we are really seeking is the balance between those activities that drain our energy and those that replenish it, wherever they may be found. This is equally relevant to our life at work (our 'worklife') and at home (our 'homelife').

---

[1] Compiled by the authors with thanks to Stephen Partridge

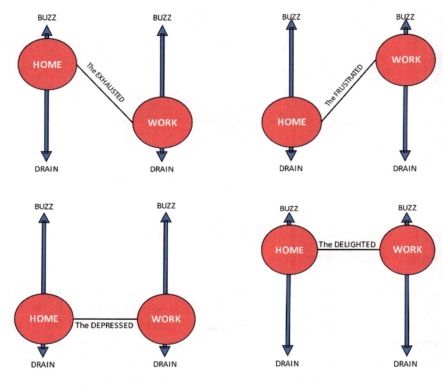

Fig. 6.2 The four scenarios

We will explore worklife in this chapter and the next to describe the possibility of a new balance. Chapter 11 touches on the home. Whereas work-life balance makes little sense, 'worklife' balance is key to being happy and fulfilled at work in the longer term and sustainably.

6.3 What's the Difference Between Work and a Hobby?

Homo sapiens, as the name suggests, is a learning animal. Throughout our working lives, we have the opportunity to develop as individuals. Our body of knowledge will grow as we study or when we face new and demanding challenges; we may finesse one or more professional or practical skill areas by applying our skills to real-life situations; we may develop a high competence in our dealings with other people and so on. Skills, knowledge and experience are vital to our success at work and particularly important where competition or standards are involved. This applies irrespective of whether we are a manager, a lawyer, a doctor, a builder or a chef. If market forces are not driving up standards, then imposed professional, trade or (in the case of the chef) food hygiene standards will ensure that our work attains and maintains a suitable level of proficiency.

As humans, we are also flexible. Many of the skills and knowledge we acquire and gradually hone during our working lives are 'transferable' and can be applied to many different work settings across organisations and across sectors. Consider, for example, interpersonal relationship skills, physical and mental dexterity and team working skills. But our capacity to develop and apply these high-order skills does not evaporate the moment we leave our work premises. If they belong anywhere, they belong to the individual.

Let's contrast the idea of work with a hobby. The Oxford English Dictionary defines a hobby as 'a favourite occupation or topic pursued for amusement…; an individual pursuit to which a person is unduly devoted'. A contemporary online definition (Wikipedia) gives us 'a regular activity that is done for enjoyment, typically during one's leisure time'. Hobbies are as varied as human nature is diverse. For some people, craftwork is extremely fulfilling; others play sport for fun where competition or exercise fills their spare time. Some like to work collectively in musical or theatrical ventures; others prefer solo activities such as meditation or yoga. Some prefer to be personally active creating things or doing DIY, others prefer crowds and spectate at sporting events, classical music or opera. Hobbies change as we get older and the strenuous activity of youth gives way to less dramatic alternatives yet even the elderly still find pleasure and fulfilment in hobbies, whether these are crosswords, croquet or crochet.

Whereas work is a professional activity carried out for financial gain, hobbies, by contrast, define us as an amateur in that field. The joy of a hobby is being in total personal control of what we do and able to set our own standards of achievement; to knock points off our golf handicap, to learn that tricky guitar riff, to lift our best weight in the gym, to hone our top-spin lob or cycle up the hill to the market without having to get off and push. Being an amateur gives us the freedom to develop at our own speed and in our own way.

Popular usage of 'amateur' suggests poor standards, inconsistent application or dilettante attitudes but dictionary definitions offer 'one who loves or has a taste for anything' reflecting the French origins of the word (as 'lover of') or even the earlier Latin root that had us all chanting at school '*amo, amas, amat*': the verb to love. An amateur undertakes a pursuit for the sheer love of it. No goals are externally set, no timescales or quality standards imposed, there is no obligatory compliance. Hobbies are relatively free and unconstrained, limited only by their cost or the amount of time and other resources available.

Our hobbies sustain us and nourish us when we have time to ourselves. They are more than mere pastimes: they matter to us far more than that. The way we spend free time outside of maintaining a home and family will show quite clearly the things to which we are drawn, because those are the things we love. The things we love to do are those to which we are devoted and to which we willingly give our time and energy, spending an extra hour getting something we're 'working' on just right. A friend of younger days used to spend his weekend carefully taking to bits the engine of his Honda motorbike and then putting it all together again. Imagine if that were his work: it would be regarded as dull and repetitive, even abusive to ask anyone to undertake a futile, circular and unproductive activity. But the fact that this was his motorbike, which he loved, made the activity a pleasure and he chose to do it.

If a hobby proves too difficult or demanding, or we are not making the degree of progress we have set ourselves, we are likely to drop it in favour of something else. In this case, it is as if we fall out of love with our chosen hobby and switch to something else as the recipient of our time and devotion. The key point is that these are our personal choices.

A quick analysis of the skill set involved in pursuing a hobby shows that we use a blend of our developed skill set: the same type of skills used in the workplace. Motor skills (in sport, playing a musical instrument), critical reasoning/logic in solving puzzles, giving fine attention in craftwork, collaborative working with others in team sport, charitable volunteering, in theatrical or music ensembles, all use some of the life skill set we have acquired. If we contrast that same skill set and put them in the workplace, the emphasis and context may be different, but the skills are basically the same or come from the same source. The critical difference between going to work and having a hobby seems to be between being obligated to (go to work) and wanting to (engage in a favourite hobby). Tony Bennet, the immensely hard-working American singer who performed well in his 80s, once famously said that he so loved singing and performing that he had never done a day's work in his life, ignoring the years of practice and rehearsal that resulted in his fame and fortune. It is a matter of attitude and perception, freedom and choice, love and devotion.

Our inner state determines how we perceive and tackle what we do. If we believe we are free to choose what we do, whether at work or elsewhere, we are likely not to feel its pressures as acutely as when we believe our choices to be constrained or determined by others. It is also likely that, if we tackle tasks with the gusto of a true enthusiast, we will draw positive reactions from those around us. This is a theme to which we will return in later chapters.

6.4　Seeking Balance in Our Life at Work

Tiredness is not simply caused by doing too much work but by doing too much of the wrong kind of work: the work that is not fulfilling. An hour of work we hate causes more tiredness, creates more wear and tear and takes more out of us than an hour of the work we love. The old saying goes that time flies when you're having fun. The same is true at work.

For one of us (David), leading programmes of Executive Education is a real joy and so he became Professor in Leadership past the usual retirement age. Those dynamic discussions with successful and able executives at Henley, Oxford and Harvard Business Schools come to mind. It is stimulating, creative and satisfying to take a brief from a client organisation and turn it into a programme for executives from the client company. Clients can be demanding; finding the right contributors can be a challenge; creating the right flow between the sessions is not straightforward but the satisfaction comes when the design is not just approved but enthusiastically welcomed by the senior players who have commissioned it. The more they are involved, the more difficult to please because they really care about the programme, the greater the effort required but also the greater the reward and the better the programme.

Clients from ICA, the Swedish retailer, have always been like this. Yet, when they are convinced that we have worked together with them to get the design right, their enthusiasm increases exponentially and they are proud of their part in making the design imaginative, relevant and coherent. They bring out the best in all of us. Similarly, during the programme, the participants play their parts in turning a good programme into a great one when they feel stimulated by it, challenged by it and energised by it. At Oxford and Henley, we can put on a 'good' programme every time, but we can only get to 'great' when the participants become co-creators of the experience every day. When that happens, the days are long (typically 12+ hour days from breakfast until after dinner) comprising 8 hours of education and another 4 hours of client contact in one form or another. But the time literally flies by, the week seems like a day or two and the end of the programme comes far too soon for all.

Amazingly, those weeks require a great deal of energy and effort, but the end of each day leaves everyone wanting more and no more than a little tired. It is not a matter of adrenalin creating nervous energy, but of stimulation becoming almost self-sustaining. Of course, tiredness sets in and most of us sleep extremely soundly at the end of such a day, but this is no drudge: it is a pleasure. In education, as in physics, perpetual motion is not possible to achieve but regenerative energy use can happen and effort is sustainable beyond what most people might imagine possible. This is not fortitude; it is more like recycling: energy expended in this way generates a great deal of new energy to do more and joy mitigates the potential strain. It is Tesla-like regenerative engine braking.

At the end of such a fully engaged week, we all return to our homes and families, not to be put back together again but bubbling over with energy to share and life to be enjoyed with our loved ones. This is not a narcotic though it can be addictive. It is not illegal, immoral or fattening, but it is life-affirming. It feels good for the soul. Musicians, sports players, chefs and actors are familiar with this, and we are unsurprised when we hear of their similar stories. Yet artisans, clinicians, restaurateurs and any manager or worker who is doing the work they love can experience the same provided they are not pushed (too far) by others.

6.5 Career Choice and Daily Choice

Certainly, days can feel long or short, work can be a joy or a drudge, we can leave our workplace elated or deflated according to our experience there. This is a huge warning to choose carefully what we do. The authors of this volume have been executive coaches and advisors for many years and we have seen how unfulfilling it has been when able individuals find themselves in the wrong kind of profession or simply in the wrong job. We came across a senior doctor who had never really wanted to do medicine but had merely drifted into it because she was a clever girl at school and the school pushed her in that direction. When, in mid-career, she paused to reflect, she realised she was trapped and seemed unable to reverse herself into a better situation. There are clear echoes here of the life transitions in Chap. 4.

Mid-life crises are complex, existential and troubling yet a key element can be the nagging question, 'is this what I'm going to be doing for the rest of my life?' A feeling of unease can result from too many days at work feeling unfulfilled. The same can be true at home but here we are concerned with the workplace. There are those who have achieved their career goals and now find they were insufficiently rewarding or merely ephemeral. There are others who realise they will never achieve their career goals and so each day at work reminds them of their frustrated ambitions. Buying a sports car or taking a career break (a gap year) may seem tempting but costly personal experience suggests that the money might be better spent since no solution is found that way (although it was a very nice car!) In the context of life transitions more broadly, mid-life crises are specific examples of a broader and more frequent experience in which transitions are difficult. A mid-life crisis is likely to be a difficulty letting go of the 'youth' stage.

So much for career choice, but annual or even daily choices at work may be treated similarly. Any job seems to have core elements that must be done. Teachers must prepare lessons, teach and mark exams. Accountants must prepare budgets, draw up accounts and stay up to date with tax changes. Street cleaners must be out in all weathers, deal with the public and clear up other people's offensive messes. Vicars must preach, conduct marriages, funerals and christenings.

When we are thinking uncreatively about such matters, we confuse the daily activities involved in a job with its purpose and meaning and can overlook opportunities to serve the purpose in other ways. However, within each job, there are choices to be made and within each day. The choices are of three distinct kinds: what we do, how we do it and our attitudes to it all. What if we could pick and choose those elements of our work we do, leaving behind those that we do not enjoy? Would that make a difference? Almost certainly, it would. Thinking more creatively, could two or three vicars decide together that one would do the weddings, another the christenings and another the funerals? Maybe, but who knows? Has anyone tried to do that? Could two managers who do not receive enough feedback from their boss try arranging to observe each other and provide feedback for each other? Could a team of painters and decorators divide up their work differently so that each could do more of what they enjoy the most? Thinking creatively in this way, it may be possible to influence the balance of what we do each day, or at least for a while.

Similarly, we may be able to influence how we do our work. Working from home, choosing our working hours, the order in which tasks are tackled are all examples of choices many of us can make and are doing so increasingly in the context of the 2020 pandemic. More deeply, we may also be able to choose our attitudes to our work and our feelings about it.

At the request of Rod Eddington, the CEO at the time, a staff satisfaction survey was conducted at British Airways throughout the month of September 2001. That was the month of 9/11 when the twin towers of the World Trade Centre in New York were destroyed by terrorists. Informal analysis of the data revealed a surprising discovery: that staff morale was greater after the disaster than before it happened. It seemed that, having seen a real and shocking disaster unfold to incredulous millions around the world, a sense of perspective was created even in an airline in which everyone knew that their business would be terribly badly affected by the impact of the attacks and staff could lose their jobs. In such a context, their current niggles and concerns seemed to pale into relative insignificance.

Thus, attitudes were changed. In this case, by external events but anyone who has experienced a significant personal loss or severe trauma tends to acquire a new sense of perspective. It is almost as if an ECT shock had been administered, one which brings about a sudden awakening to new possibilities or at least a much clearer vision. The possibility arises, that we may be able to shift our attitudes and see matters in greater perspective by a sheer act of will. We can, at a pinch, choose how we face the circumstances before us whether they appear positive or negative at first glance. We may, with Rudyard Kipling, be able to face triumph and disaster and treat those two imposters just the same. We may be able to choose what we do, how we do it and how we feel about it. In the next chapters, we will explore these possibilities and offer a tool to help bring them into use.

6.6 Summary and Conclusion

Seeking balance between work and life is a logical impossibility since work is such an important part of life. One is entirely contained within the other. Maintaining a healthy balance between work and home seems a challenge for many of us. There are many examples of the exhausted, the frustrated, the depressed and the delighted, and all of them may be missing a related and equally important alternative: to seek the balance between those elements of our work that give us joy and those that destroy or deplete it. This is to seek balance in our life at work, or, for that matter, at home. In order to attain balance in our worklife or homelife, we need to consider what we do, how we do it and how we feel about it, exercising choices at each level: career, annual or daily.

7

Analysing Worklife

There are aspects of our experience at work that make us feel better and others that make us feel worse. In this chapter, we will consider how these dynamics work, how they affect us and how we can analyse them. This is the start of 'job crafting'. We will explain and elaborate more on this in the next chapter.

The analysis begins by identifying the discrete elements of our work. Each may then be weighted and its impact assessed. It is not a precise measurement but a subjective estimate of the effect on us so that we can make comparisons and reveal what is happening. It also raises the possibility that some of these elements might be changed or reconsidered. The first task is to break down what is happening into its constituent parts and consider each separately.

7.1 Elements of Our Worklife

Whether we are feeling down about our work or ecstatic about it, we tend to allow this strong overall impression to fuse all the elements or our work together in our minds. This aggregation is unhelpful to our

Table 7.1 Elements of each job

Supermarket manager	University lecturer	General practitioner (GP)
Dealing with customers	Preparing and giving lectures	Consulting with patients face to face
Managing staff	Marking assignments	Telephone consultations
Working in a team and leading it	Applying for research grants	Making house calls
Dealing with complaints	Giving seminars and tutorials	Writing referrals to hospital doctors
Solving problems	Doing research	Keeping up to date with clinical research
Working evenings and weekends	Supervision of research assistants	Management of the practice
Ensuring profitable operation	Writing and publishing	Training and supervising junior doctors
Managing profitable growth	Pastoral care of tutees	Conducting research

analytical purpose here. We need to break down our work into its constituent parts to understand and address it. Let us consider three examples, noting eight elements of each job in Table 7.1.[1]

These lists are subjectively constructed rather than formal elements of a job description. The elements are potentially different for different people in the same job. If our general practitioner is young and single, then working long hours may not enter his or her consciousness as a relevant element of the job to consider. If he or she is older, married and with children, it might well be an important and problematic matter. For our university lecturer, supervision of research assistants may not be worth a second thought but for a lecturer who has never considered herself in a leadership or management role, this may prove to be a stressor and a real turn-off. Our supermarket manager may consider working in a team and leading it as two separate subjects unless, that is, he or she finds that membership and leadership clash and it is the need to do both simultaneously, which is the problem to think through.

The subjectivity of the lists will extend to how many elements are considered and which they are. For many of us, a few issues seem to

---

[1] All tables in this chapter are compiled by the authors.

dominate. They are forceful features in a broad landscape and seem to obscure the rest. For others everything seems to be connected, and it is hard to distinguish discrete elements for consideration. Breaking the job into its constituent parts is the antidote to the aggregation mentioned above and helps to see matters more clearly. This may take a little time and thought, or even some help from others who are more distant from the issues.

For our purposes in this chapter, the length of the lists and the specific elements used are immaterial. We are concerned with their impact on the person who is compiling the list for him/herself. The first question to ask of any element is: on balance, is the effect of this aspect of the work positive, negative or neutral? In other words, does the element give energy, take it away or have no discernible effect? Related to this: how great is the impact? A positive impact may be slightly amusing or a huge source of delight; a negative impact could be a mild irritation or a game-changing, gut-wrenching drudge. Finally, how frequently is each encountered? A mild irritation encountered infrequently is minute in comparison with a frequent or constant heart-sink.

Initially, the size of the impact can be a blend of intensity and frequency. In addition, to keep scaling issues to a minimum, let us use a scale that goes from minus 10 to plus 10 so that comparisons can be made, although this slightly and temporarily constrains the way we use the scale.

Let us consider in Table 7.2 the case of our restaurant manager, Ella:

Ella is bright, bubbly, warm and friendly. She loves dealing with customers, even dealing with their complaints, because then she has an opportunity to delight them and impress them with her flexibility, charm and willingness to be helpful. Her role is clear and she believes this is a real strength of hers, turning customers into fans and advocates who tell their friends: she effectively recruits them into the advertising department! Solving problems is rather less impactful but she believes in her own ingenuity and is always willing to listen to others. On the one hand, she considers ensuring profitable operation as a form of problem-solving, maximising efficiency and gaining quality without undue expense. On the other hand, Ella dislikes the ambiguity and complexity of being, at

Table 7.2 Ella's job elements

Supermarket manager Ella	On balance: positive/negative/neutral?	Size of impact (intensity/frequency combined)
Dealing with customers	Positive (+)	8
Managing staff	Negative (−)	5
Working in a team and leading it	Negative (−)	7
Dealing with complaints	Positive (+)	9
Solving problems	Positive (+)	3
Working evenings and weekends	Neutral (+/−)	0
Ensuring profitable operation	Positive (+)	5
Managing profitable growth	Negative (−)	5

the same time, a member and leader of a team and finds managing staff stressful. Her role here is somewhat unclear, especially with the head of finance who is better paid than her and whose skills she depends upon. Finally, she is an unconfident marketer so she is fine managing a profitable operation but not with managing profitable growth, given her current state of knowledge of marketing. Hence the various scores in the table.

Incidentally, if we do the maths, we can see that, for Ella, her job is positive on balance. The positive elements add up to an impact of +25 and that compares with −17 for the negative elements to give a net score of +8. Yet the negative elements are significant, as we can see and, whilst Ella is in positive territory, I would fear for her employer that the negatives might drive her away to another role where the net positive balance is greater.

These issues are not intrinsic to being a supermarket manager; they are to do with Ella as an individual in the role. Consider another manager of the same supermarket, Gavin. Gavin is a different kind of manager who stays somewhat more in the background and pushes his team forward because he is rather shy, though he has considerable social skills he can bring out when required and he is very robust emotionally so conflict

Table 7.3 Gavin's job elements

Supermarket manager Gavin	On balance: positive/negative/neutral?	Size of impact (intensity/frequency combined)
Dealing with customers	+/–	0
Managing staff	+	7
Working in a team and leading it	+	3
Dealing with complaints	–	5
Solving problems	+	7
Working evenings and weekends	+/–	0
Ensuring profitable operation	+	3
Managing profitable growth	+	6

does not faze him. He can deal with customers but finds this tiring as it is not his natural game. He takes pride in empowering his assistant managers to take the lead with customers while he ensures the team is in good shape, morale is high and conflict is eliminated one way or another. He has been a food and beverage manager in a large hotel and, before that, did a degree in marketing. He might score the elements differently as in Table 7.3:

On balance, Gavin's experience of the same elements in the job put him well into positive territory: +26 compares with just –5 for a net score of +21. Gavin seems to be thriving in the role because he is differently equipped compared with Ella and plays the role differently also. He might additionally replace some of these elements or add others to the list. So might Ella. But in the current circumstances, we can see that the job looks different to our two supermarket managers before they do anything to change it.

Working in this way, we are attempting to make a note of the significant elements of the job as we see them personally and irrespective of what others say about the role. The list of elements: how many items are included, their nature and what we call them are all up to us. Their impact ratings are equally personal. The point is twofold: to externalise the issues, which brings benefits in itself (see below), and to represent, as best we can, how the job looks and feels to us to enable analysis. These elements are selected from our personal perspective and may include other factors which are not tasks or duties such as:

- My relationship with my boss
- Feeling appreciated by my clients
- The outlook for the company
- The amount and nature of the changes happening in my work
- The location of the company and its surroundings
- The company's reputation

Representing the look and feel of the job in our personal experience is an obvious thing to do. But why should we go through this formal, systematic process of externalising the issues by writing them down? Why not just think about them? The answer comes from neuroscience research. In the words of Matthew Lieberman and colleagues in their 2007 research paper on the subject:

> When you put feelings into words, you're activating this prefrontal region [of the brain] and seeing a reduced response in the amygdala the same way you hit the brake when you are driving when you see an orange yellow light, when you put feelings into words, you seem to be hitting the brakes on your emotional responses.

The very act of putting them on paper (or, presumably, typing them into a file online) causes our brain to respond more rationally. By disrupting our emotional responses, we facilitate analytical thought and begin to develop a greater capacity to deal with the matter: just by writing it down! So, rather than this being a chore, it begins to have a positive impact immediately. This works when we are thinking through any matter that is troubling us, incidentally, and therapists, counsellors and coaches often deploy the same tactic of *externalisation* to create a measure of distance and stop the matter from having such control over us. So, we advocate writing all the key elements down, good and bad.

7.2 Exercise

So maybe we should try this out, not theoretically but for real. Here is a template to use:

What is your job?

Write the elements of your job here, in your own words	On balance is each element positive, negative or neutral?	How big is the impact from 1-10? (Intensity and frequency combined)
When you add up all the positive and negative scores, what is the NET SCORE?		

We guess that this did not take you long, since these matters tend to be relatively clear in our minds, though it may seem unusual to set them out in this way. There are no right or wrong ways of doing this: it simply needs to reflect an accurate and honest picture of the way you experience your work. Two colleagues may use different elements to describe the same job because their experiences of it are different and unique to themselves.

Now, working with your own results, we can start to ask questions about what you have described.

> 1. What is your net score? Are you describing work that is more positive than negative or is it the reverse? What are your thoughts and feelings about that?

2. What are the dominant elements? You will have scored these highest, whether positive or negative. You might want to make a note of why this is so, again externalising the issues here. Start with the mostpowerful impacts and work here with just the top two or three in order to become focused. Take particular note of the frequency with which these things occur in your work.

3. Reflect creatively on how you might create change in your work by changing the elements in some way. Could new positive element be introduced? Could some of the negative elements be removed? Could you change the frequency with which these things occur? Could you combine elements in some way so that the negative impact of some issues are diluted by the positive impact of others?

7.3 A Worked Example

Returning to the University lecturer from earlier, let's call her Carol. You will recall that she listed relevant elements of her job as in Table 7.4, to which we have added her impact ratings:

The positive elements of her job aggregate to a score of +21 and the negative to −16: a fine balance. At a glance, the issues are crystal clear, at least on the surface. Carol loves to teach and finds the preparation and giving of lectures, seminars and tutorials are very positive aspects of the role. Similarly, doing the research keeps her up to date. She sees herself primarily as an educator. Applying for research grants is a necessary drudge, but she is often buoyed by the prospect of actually doing the research if the grant comes through. Pastoral care is reasonably satisfying but hard for her as she finds the role time-consuming and sometimes feels the students are complaining without good cause. She accepts that she needs to supervise research assistants but, since she is not very assertive, she finds this somewhat stressful. However, marking assignments is purgatory for her. She finds it rather depressing that the students do not seem to share her enthusiasm for her subject, nor do they seem to understand it very well and constantly correcting their essays gets her down. By contrast, writing and publishing give her pride that she is contributing to

Table 7.4 Carol's job elements

University lecturer in education Carol	Positive/negative/neutral?	Impact
Preparing and giving lectures	+	9
Marking assignments	−	7
Applying for research grants	+/−	0
Giving seminars and tutorials	+	7
Doing research	+	3
Supervision of research assistants	−	6
Writing and publishing	+	2
Pastoral care of tutees	−	3
Net score	+5	

her subject, though the slow pace at which these publications come out and the pressure from her university for her to publish take the shine off this activity for her. Carol might answer the questions above as follows:

> 1. Adding up the positive impacts and the negative impacts, are you describing work that is more positive than negative or is it the reverse? What are your thoughts and feelings about that?
>
> *I knew that all was not well in my role but had not realised how finely balanced it all is. I've always wanted to be a university lecturer, so I am surprised and disappointed that I am not having a better time at work when I am doing what I've always wanted to do.*
>
> 2. What are the dominant elements? You will have scored these highest, whether positive or negative. You might want to make a note of why this is so, again externalising the issues here. Start with the most powerful impacts and work here with just the top two or three in order to become focused. Take particular note of the frequency with which these things occur.
>
> GIVING LECTURES, SEMINARS AND TUTORIALS +9 AND +7
>
> *This is what I have always wanted to do and I love it. It is a joy every day to express my enthusiasm for my subject to all the students in my classes. Many respond positively and ask great questions. They make me laugh and it does me good. These are the times I am sure I'm doing the right job for me.*
>
> MARKING ASSIGNMENTS -7
>
> *Marking assignments is rather tedious and quite depressing. I seem to read endless rehashes of my own lectures and find it frustrating that the students are not reading around the subject. It is also frustrating when they seem to have no more than a partial grasp of most of the concepts I have been getting them to think about, although when a really able student reads broadly and writes well, it can be a joy to read and mark his or her work. I seem to have a pile of marking to do most weeks but this is because I set them so many essays, as was the norm at my university when I was a student.*
>
> SUPERVISION OF RESEARCH ASSISTANTS -6
>
> *The problem here is simple: I often can't get them to do what I want them to do. Our research progresses slowly because my team members are quite slack in their use of time and seem not to be very organised, even though they do seem to get the work done eventually.*

3. Reflect creatively on how you might create change in your work by changing the elements in some way. Could new positive elements be introduced? Could some of the negative elements be removed? Could you change the frequency with which these things occur? Could you combine elements in some way so that the negative impact of some issues is diluted by the positive impact of others?

LECTURES, SEMINARS AND TUTORIALS + 9 and +7

I'm good at this and I don't need to do anything to continue enjoying it. Though I'm now beginning to think that I may need to focus more on the seminars and tutorials where I can check the students' understanding more and encourage them more to read around the subject.

MARKING ASSIGNMENTS -7 (Could go to 0)

Looking at this more objectively, it is clear that I am the one who is simply setting too many assignments in the first place and maybe that is causing my students to do the minimum for each essay or project. I can set fewer and give each greater weighting in the evaluation scheme. I could also try to make each assignment more practical and less academic to capture their enthusiasm for the possibilities they are working with.

SUPERVISION OF RESEARCH ASSISTANTS -6 (Possibly 0 or even +3)

As an enthusiast about my subject, I am conscious that I have recruited onto my research team, other enthusiasts. They are not especially hard working or organised, though they know a great deal about our research topics. As this grant is coming to an end, and the new grant is in a somewhat different field, I am minded to switch my recruitment strategy. I will try this time to recruit organised and disciplined, conscientious researchers. If they know little about our subject at the start, I will teach them about it and they will learn fast. I can see this could transform my experience of research supervision and this could take the impact of this aspect of my work to a neutral or even positive score.

7.4 Reactive or Proactive?

The examples provided here have all been reactive: dealing with issues or opportunities as they arise. Naturally, there is a proactive version of this. Having conducted an initial analysis of the situation, it would be possible to review the entire picture and decide how you would like it to look: the ideal scores that could send you home happy and energised. This would require an analysis of each score and a decision taken about the balance of the job you would most like to create. This would not be a Pollyanna fantasy in which everything was blissful but rather a realistic best case that would feel good on balance.

Table 7.5 Steve's job elements now

General practitioner (GP) Steve	Positive/negative/neutral?	Impact
Consulting with patients face to face	+	6
Telephone/video consultations	+/−	0
Making house calls	+	7
Writing referrals to hospital doctors	−	2
Keeping up to date with clinical research	+	6
Management of the practice	−	9
Training and supervising junior doctors	−	6
Conducting research	+	4
Net score	+6	

We can use our General Practitioner (GP) as an example to consider in this way. Let us call him Steve and first show how he might score his working world (Table 7.5).

Steve qualified in medicine roughly ten years ago. He had always wanted to be a doctor as science appealed to him greatly. He loved the precision of much of the hard science and the challenge of applying it to the messier world of patient care. He greatly enjoyed his relationship with his patients and the thought that he could make a significant difference in their lives, either through helping them get well if they were sick or simply helping them make positive choices about their health and that of their family. He liked to think that he was a good doctor and the feedback from the patients seemed to confirm that. He had not always wanted to be a GP, however. He had considered a career in clinical research or in psychiatry but opted for general practice because he could see opportunities to incorporate his other interests into his role as a GP. He thrived on the challenge of getting to know, or, better still, to understand his patients and took an interest in them from first contact, through their various episodes of illness and life stages through which he saw, and occasionally, helped them pass.

There were two roles, however, into which he had 'fallen' rather than chosen more actively. The first was becoming a trainer of junior doctors (registrars). He took over temporarily when his partner went on maternity leave and had consoled himself that this would just be temporary because he didn't enjoy the supervisory role and the teaching that went with it. He had become trapped in the role when his partner resigned from the practice, opting to be a stay-at-home mum for the first few years of her daughter's life. The second was the management of the practice. The tradition in the practice was that the most senior partner led and managed the practice, and he had joined a practice or four partners as a young fifth partner with much older colleagues. In his ten years, the other partners had all retired, one of them taking early retirement so the senior partner role had been thrust upon him.

When thinking about how he would really like his experience of work to be, he scored it like this (Table 7.6):

Steve has come to realise that he could have choices if he could reposition himself in the practice. First, he has realised that he does not have to continue as a trainer of the registrar. He could talk to his partners to convert Maggie's interest in training into becoming the trainer/supervisor of the registrars. This is a better solution than having the practice stop training since that would have income implications and they would lose the extra pair of hands a registrar provided. He could help out occasionally but not be the designated trainer. Second, he could break with tradition and appoint his colleague Sian as the practice leader. He knows that Sian is young but has strong managerial capabilities and he could shadow her, mentor her, coach her, in order to give her the confidence to step up to the leadership role somewhat ahead of schedule.

What is more, he could then make much more time for research. He had always felt guilty about his spending time on research because of his conscientious attention to the roles he did not enjoy. But, liberated by a new set of expectations of his partnership contributions, he could indulge

Table 7.6 Steve's job elements ideally

General practitioner (GP) Steve	Positive/negative/neutral?	Impact
Consulting with patients face to face	+	8
Telephone/video consultations	+	2
Making house calls	+	7
Writing referrals to hospital doctors	−	2
Keeping up to date with clinical research	+	8
Management of the practice	−	2
Training and supervising junior doctors	−	1
Conducting research	+	8
Net score	+28	

his research interests starting with a project on telephone/video consultations which would increase his interest in those too. Of course, he then needed to sound out Maggie and Sian specifically and the other two partners in general but he could see a better fit not just for him but for the others also.

7.5 Summary and Conclusion

In order to take control of our experience of work, we have first to understand its dynamics. We have to break it into its constituent parts and evaluate each in terms of its impact. Having done so, it is possible to reimagine our roles and how we would like them to be, planning a transition and ultimately intervening to change our experience of work until it suits us better. This process starts with a careful analysis and leads to focused action.

Reference

Lieberman, M. D., Eisenberger, N. I., Crockett, M. J., Tom, S. M., Pfeifer, J. H., & Way, B. M. (2007). Putting feelings into words. Affect labeling disrupts amygdala activity in response to affective stimuli. *Psychological Science, 18*(5), 421–428.

8

Job Crafting

Previous chapters described a need for us to '*seek the balance between those elements of our work that give us joy and those that destroy or deplete it*'. Here we propose 'Job Crafting' as a mechanism to achieve this alongside multiple other positive outcomes. It is employee-driven and used to make the jobs employees have into the jobs they want. It is a variant and extension of the technique outlined in the previous chapter.

Job crafting enables employees to re-engineer their roles into a format that better works for them by amending three key areas: what they do, who they do it with and why they do it. In turn, job crafting provides employees with a tool to maximise their 'buzzes' and reduce their 'drains'. The practice has consistently been found to improve a range of work-related outcomes which benefit employees and employers alike. These include improvements in well-being, motivation, happiness and engagement among many more.

Whilst the concept of job crafting is not new and over 20 years of academic research exists on the topic, interest in the benefits of its application has only recently taken off. It has gained considerable traction with leaders, HR practitioners and employees alike and is used in a wide variety of organisations internationally.

In this chapter we will review the pressures and shifts in mindset which have led to the evolution of job crafting. We will also take a deep dive into what job crafting looks like in practice, why and how people craft, and what we need to consider when doing so. Since this field is relatively new, we will document the research reasonably thoroughly so that the interested reader can follow up any interest generated in the field.

8.1 The Evolution of Job Design; from Top-Down to Bottom-Up

Jobs encompass the constellation of tasks and interpersonal relationships assigned to individuals at work. The design of this constellation is controlled through the process of job design, which manages how jobs are structured and executed. Typically, a 'one size fits all' approach has been adopted, with the same job descriptions being assigned to multiple employees sharing roles with the same or similar titles. At times, changes to individuals or the context of jobs may mean the initial job design assigned to an employee via their job description is no longer suitable and needs to be changed. This is where job re-design comes into play. It also represents the evolution from job-centred role descriptions to person-centred role descriptions.

Job re-design typically occurs for one of two reasons: to adapt to changing contextual requirements or to improve individual motivation and performance. Traditionally, the process of job design and re-design is a top-down process, guided by technical and HR considerations with little input from the employees whose jobs are being re-designed. Theirs is a passive role. Over time it could be argued that these classic approaches to job re-design have become increasingly less fit for purpose, especially in the context of the modern workplace. Indeed, academics and practitioners now recognise that, in the context of the uncertain, ever-changing and complex constellation of elements that come to form contemporary jobs, traditional job descriptions soon become outdated. Roles change and evolve at such a pace that employees' original job design and related job descriptions fail to reflect current reality soon after they are produced and become increasingly disconnected from reality over time.

In addition to the challenges described, a notable power shift has also taken place across the twentieth century with regard to the distribution of employees' power, as described in Pendleton and Furnham's (2016; Pendleton, Furnham, & Cowell, 2021) guide to leadership. This shift sees a move from the traditional thinking of employer domination and employee subordination to leadership which focuses on building and sustaining an employee-employer partnership. In addition, it can be argued that the top-down nature of these classic approaches also insufficiently meets employees' increasing expectations to feel involved and consulted at work (as described in earlier chapters). In doing so, they also miss a key opportunity to capture and incorporate employees' specialist role knowledge into the job re-design process and take account of individual differences and needs.

8.2 The Rise of Employeeship and Job Crafting

We see this shift in thinking reflected in new philosophies and approaches to leadership which seek to empower and involve employees, and to create 'employeeship' as a complement to leadership.

Employeeship: a management philosophy which aims to create a culture of ownership and responsibility across all employees in an organisation.

The philosophy is described as '*medarbetarskap*' in Sweden where it has most commonly been adopted and researched. Employeeship challenges traditional, top-down approaches to leadership and introduces a complementary bottom-up element. Employeeship aims to create partnerships between managers and employees in which they work together to take mutual responsibility for, involvement in, and ownership of, their work. The whole approach is designed holistically to engage the workforce and to promote openness, honesty, responsibility and trust.

The shift towards progressive leadership philosophies like employeeship is also evident in modern approaches to managing teams. For example, we increasingly see organisations and managers taking steps to empower teams and encourage them to decide which team members take on each task, and how they go about these. Modern approaches to job re-design are required to meet employee expectations, and to future-proof organisations in the face of the inevitable change they will face. Of the modern approaches which have emerged, we believe job crafting provides the most promise.

Job crafting has evolved from traditional forms of job re-design; however, its key difference is that it is an employee-driven process. In the world of increasingly shared leadership, this bottom-up approach turns traditional approaches to job re-design on their head. It shifts the responsibility for job design, which originally fell to managers, into employees' hands. This enables a subject expert to guide the job re-design process. The incumbent is likely to be the person most familiar with the complex constellation of elements that form the job, the contextual challenges faced in the role and the nature of the person completing that job: namely, themselves! In addition, this 'DIY' approach to job re-design enables employees to be proactive in shaping their roles and how they perform them. Job crafting embodies and operationalises the principles of employeeship by providing employees with a chance to exercise ownership and responsibility over their roles and contributions.

This modern approach enables a move from static job designs imposed on employees to those which are dynamic, ever-evolving and guided by employee-input. Such malleability may not only make it possible for organisations to react more effectively to the constant change faced in the modern workplace but also better recognise and play to the individual differences that we know exist between employees.

Public interest in job crafting is increasingly gaining traction and growing over time. This is reflected in the data provided by Google Trends which highlighted how the interest in Job Crafting, indicated by searches for the term, peaked and remained high between 2004 and 2007, the period in which the seminal research papers were released. After a short lull in interest following this period, interest in job crafting now continues to build over time towards its original peak. Figure 8.1 is below, data source: Google Trends (https://www.google.com/trends).

The practical application of job crafting has also taken off and is adopted by employees globally across a vast range of occupations,

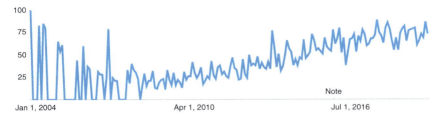

Fig. 8.1 Job crafting Google searches. (*Interest over time: Numbers represent search interest relative to the highest point on the chart for the given region and time. A value of 100 is the peak popularity for the term. A value of 50 means that the term is half as popular. A score of 0 means there was not enough data for this term*)

industries and levels of seniority. Job crafting has also caught the interest of organisations and HR practitioners alike and is now being deployed within organisations including Google, Facebook, McKinsey, Intel, Virgin and KPMG.

8.3 Job Crafting in Practice

We have discussed how job crafting is a bottom-up approach to job re-design, but how do employees put it into practice? The following definitions are of use when explaining what job crafting entails:

> Job crafting is 'an employee-initiated approach which enables employees to shape their own work environment such that it fits their individual needs'. (Tims & Bakker, 2010)

> Job crafting entails 'the active changes employees make to their own job designs in ways that can bring about numerous positive outcomes, including increased engagement, job satisfaction, person-job-fit, psychological empowerment, resilience, and thriving'. (Berg et al., 2008)

At its core, 'job crafting' describes the proactive actions employees take to personalise their jobs in ways which make them better aligned with their individual interests, strengths and values. Job crafting succeeds in helping employees transform the elements which form their current jobs into the jobs they love. It is a self-initiated process, and employees are driven to craft by three key sources of motivation (Wrzesniewski & Dutton, 2001; Wrzesniewski et al., 2003):

1. A need for personal control
2. A need to promote a positive sense of self
3. A need for interaction and connection with other people

The most popular example of job crafting originates from research conducted by Amy Wrzesniewski, Jane Dutton and Gelaye Debebe from the University of Michigan (2016). They sought to understand how employees feel about conducting what is sometimes seen as the 'dirty work' in organisations. This term is used to describe work which is low-paid, non-technical and often perceived to be arduous and unrewarding. To investigate this, they spoke to cleaning staff within a hospital and asked them to tell them their stories about their working experience there. They asked them about what they did every day, how they experienced their work and how they felt about it.

From these conversations, two distinct groups emerged. The first described their jobs exactly as one would predict based on the academic literature regarding this kind of work; they didn't say it was very satisfying or high skilled, but they said they were motivated to complete the work for remuneration and the tasks they said matched those on the job description exactly.

By contrast, the other group of cleaners spoke about their work in a completely different manner. They described their work as enjoyable, meaningful and said they felt it was highly skilled. Most notably, when asked about what they did at work, they described a set of tasks completely different to those described by cleaners in the first group. For example, they described noting which patients appeared lonely or downbeat during their initial cleaning rounds. Later they re-visited and spent time talking to them in an attempt to cheer them up. Another member of staff told the researchers that, when cleaning the unit which cared for non-responsive patients, they would frequently amend the position and layout of the paintings hung on the walls in the hope that even by altering a small part of the patients' physical environment, they may be able to stimulate them. Others even risked being fired when they tried to relieve patients' concerns about elderly visitors getting lost by chaperoning them back through the labyrinthine layout of the hospital to their cars.

The researchers were perplexed by how such vast differences could exist between these two groups of staff in terms of how they viewed and conducted their work. To investigate, they reviewed which areas of the hospital the groups worked in, what their shift patterns were, and which members of staff they frequently interacted with. The researchers found no differences between the two groups on these dimensions. Still perplexed, they asked the staff in the second group whether these additional activities were part of their jobs and one response stood out as they replied: 'that's not part of my job. But that's part of me'.

On reflection, it became clear to the researchers that they had uncovered a phenomenon. The second group of staff were approaching and conducting their jobs in their own way. They were doing this without the knowledge of the hospital management, and sometimes even went as far as breaking the rules to do so. The practice these staff had undertaken to reimagine and redefine their roles in a way which better suited them as individuals was job crafting.

As illustrated through the example of the hospital cleaners, job crafting involves making changes to multiple aspects of employees' jobs. Research conducted since this discovery shows that job crafting is tripartite in structure and involves making changes to three key aspects of work. These include amending:

- The structure of employees' roles (*task crafting*)
- The interactions employees have at work (*relational crafting*)
- The way in which employees think about their jobs (*cognitive crafting*)

8.4 Task Crafting

The first type of crafting describes how employees shape and mould the structure and content of their roles by amending the tasks they engage in at work. This involves making changes to the number, form or scope of their tasks. In practice this can mean taking on tasks in addition to those included in the formal job description, or even removing those listed on it. Other ways in which employees can task craft include expanding or reducing the scope of tasks or changing how they are done.

In terms of the hospital cleaners, the employee who moved the paintings around the unit was engaging in task crafting by adding an additional task which expanded the scope of their tasks from cleaning to caring and thereby enriching the purpose of the work. In practice, those seeking to task craft are likely to assess their tasks and establish which give them a 'buzz' or which 'drain' them.

The extent to which these activities will energise an individual is likely in part to relate to how much they play to individuals' interests, strengths and values. For example, chefs with an artistic streak may find themselves drained by having to complete food that has been mostly prepared in advance but may find that plating up their own culinary creations in a visually appealing manner gives them a buzz. These crafters would likely seek further opportunities to combine their artistic and culinary interests at work as this energises them. They may seek to create a special dining experience which fuses art and food. In contrast, they may wish to delegate food preparation to others, or change the types of dishes they make to those which require minimal preparation as it drains them.

Another example of task crafting involves one of the authors' colleagues. The employee in question worked in a customer support function but had a passion and talent for animation and design. When the company decided to re-brand and launch a new website, he saw an opportunity to play to his strengths and interests and incorporate these into his work. Whilst there was no overlap between his role and the marketing work, he volunteered to get involved. He designed an animation which succinctly and stylishly communicated the company's core purpose and message. In so doing, he used task crafting to incorporate his interests into his work and played to his strengths while adding value to the business.

Teams can even work together to task craft collectively, frequently practised via 'task swapping'. Equipped with the often-pre-established knowledge of one another's' strengths, interests and values, teams can come together to evaluate and re-distribute tasks and responsibilities to those whose strengths, interests and values are best aligned. Over time, this practice is likely to educate others regarding team members' preferences, strengths, interests and values. This improved understanding is likely to result in better-informed work allocation and increasingly to align individuals with the work which best suits them.

This brings to mind a team in a legal firm who had a somewhat controversially named 'crap cart' that they used to task swap. Before each Monday morning team meeting, employees were asked to place a 'crap' case file onto the cart. These files related to cases which employees were not interested in or motivated by, or in which they were unable to establish a good relationship with the client. During meetings employees were given a chance to review and choose a new case from the cart. The manager originally introduced the exercise to boost team morale but found learning about individuals' unique interests and strengths to be an added benefit. Through this insight, she was able to coach and develop two of the individuals to become legal specialists and on to become partners within the firm.

8.5 Relational Crafting

Relational crafting involves re-designing and re-shaping the social environment at work by changing the relationships and interactions with others. These relationships include those that are formally assigned to employees, such as team members and managers. They also include those which employees are independently motivated to establish and sustain, such as friendships and mentoring relationships. Employees engage in relational crafting when they make changes to the type, nature, number and extent of relationships and interactions that they have with others at work.

In practice, employees are encouraged to note the interactions and relationships they have at work and reflect on how they make them feel, focusing on whether they leave them feeling drained or energised. They would seek to reduce interactions with those they find draining and maximise interactions with energising individuals. This could be achieved simply by increasing the number of interactions, for example by increasingly aligning work with theirs, or by changing the nature of such interactions, for example by inviting them to lunch or to have a coffee together. It could even be as simple as changing where someone sits in relation to others.

Employees can also engage in relational crafting using technology. For example, they may choose to minimise face-to-face interactions with others through the increasing adoption of non-direct methods of communication, such as email or instant messenger. They may utilise virtual networks such as LinkedIn or intranets to expand their networks and align themselves with others. Internet conferencing is increasingly deployed in this way to the extent that some have discovered 'Zoom fatigue', but the technology can help enormously to shift the nature of communication and relationships with colleagues, clients and associates wherever they may be located.

Others may adopt more traditional methods such as volunteering for, or joining, employee resource groups which bring employees with common interests or backgrounds together. In doing so, they are likely to gain access to like-minded individuals and find a space in which they can incorporate their *interests* into their work. Relational crafting, on the one hand, may also focus on *values*. For example, an altruistic employee who does not feel his role offers sufficient opportunities to help others could offer to mentor a junior colleague. On the other hand, relational crafting can also be used by recipients to increase their social *support* at work by seeking out mentoring relationships with those more senior to them.

A great example of how employees have used relational crafting to incorporate their personal values into their work is embodied in 'The Together Project'. This charity, based in the UK City of Bath, was formed by a group of local vets who give some of their free time to provide care to over 45 dogs owned by homeless people in the city. In doing so, these employees have not only created a new type of relationship for themselves at work but have also expanded the nature of their relationships into volunteering.

8.6 Cognitive Crafting

Cognitive crafting is not so much manifest in behaviour externally as in thoughts and feelings internally. Cognitive crafting describes how employees change their attitudes to their work, how they think and feel about it, and the meaning and purpose they find in it. By using cognitive crafting to reframe their work, employees have an impact on their feelings of self-worth, how they perceive their personal contributions to the world, to the organisation or to others. Cognitive crafting is very much 'on trend' with the twenty-first-century workforce as there has been an explosion in interest regarding how we connect to our work, especially in terms of our happiness, meaning and motivation at work.

In practice, employees commonly cognitively craft by stepping back from seeing their jobs as sets of tasks and, instead, seeing them as a collection of elements attached to a common meaning and purpose. This method was utilised by members of the hospital cleaning staff we mentioned earlier, when they were asked 'what do you do' by the researchers. Responses from the job crafting staff included '*I am an ambassador for the hospital*'. Another even replied, '*I am a healer*', because they recognised that the tasks in their role come together to play a critical role in creating the safe, clean and caring environments crucial for patient healing. They had reframed their role significantly.

A well-known example of cognitive crafting was illustrated when President John F. Kennedy visited the NASA headquarters for the first time in 1961. During his tour of the facility, he introduced himself to a janitor who was cleaning the floor and he asked him what his role was at NASA. Famously, the man responded: '*I'm helping put a man on the moon!*'

This response reflects how the janitor also looked beyond the individual tasks that comprised his role and redefined it according to the overall purpose to which he was contributing.

Another way in which employees can cognitively craft their jobs is to re-assign themselves a new job title. These titles often speak to the purpose and meaning of the role, encouraging employees to live these through their work. For example, waste collectors could re-name themselves 'community cleaners' or teachers could consider themselves 'knowledge navigators'. Organisations also appear to recognise the benefit of emphasising the purpose and meaning of work through titles. For example, we increasingly see adverts for Human Resource roles with the title of 'Happiness Director' or 'Chief happiness Officer'. These renamed roles can generate high levels of cynicism and ridicule if stretched too far. However, reimagining a role to give it greater purpose and, in that way, creating greater alignment and role satisfaction for the current or desired role holder is a significant and inexpensive benefit. In this way a team of insurers we worked with redefined their work as *safeguarding people's futures and dreams*. Similarly, exclusive jewellers Cartier use the term 'Ambassador' rather than 'sales assistant' implying these employees are there to represent the Cartier brand as much as to sell products.

> **Reflection**
>
> Take some time to reflect on your own working experience and consider the following to establish if you have ever job crafted:
> - Have you ever changed aspects of your work to complement your interests, strengths or values better?
> - Are there any tasks or relationships at work that previously drained you? What happened to them? Did you take any steps to minimise or remove these?
> - Are there any tasks or relationships at work that energise and give you a buzz? Have you done anything to preserve or increase the presence of these in your role?
> - To what extent do you get a chance to utilise your strengths and play to your interests at work? How does this happen?
> - To what extent does your work help you to fulfil your personal values and how? Were you always able to do so?
> - If you do think you have job crafted, what impact do you think this has had on you?

8.7 Why Should You Care About Job Crafting?

We predict that your responses to the previous questions will have illustrated that you have job crafted in the past! It's not only you; research covering a range of organisations, from those in the Fortune 500 to non-profits, consistently reports that employees are already job crafting. This finding has been reported across all sectors, industries and levels of seniority, and even in organisations where it is explicitly forbidden. This interest is also evidenced by the jump in online searches and the fact that large organisations are adopting the practice. Since it is being adopted and has the potential fundamentally to change employees' jobs structurally, interpersonally and cognitively, we must ensure we understand the practice. This is the first reason we should care about job crafting.

Secondly, we should care because job crafting is a win-win process for employees and employers alike. Indeed, findings show it positively impacts a host of work-related outcomes which mutually benefit employees and the organisations for which they work.

Cross-sectional analyses show positive correlations between job crafting and employees' levels of engagement, organisational commitment, job satisfaction, well-being, performance and happiness (Bakker et al., 2012; Ghitulescu, 2007; Leana et al., 2009; Van Wingerden & Poell, 2017). Even more encouragingly, studies show improvements over long periods of time in employees' levels of engagement, well-being, positive affect, self-efficacy and in-role performance after they engage in job crafting (Gordon et al., 2018; Van den Heuvel et al., 2015; Van Wingerden et al., 2017a; Van Wingerden et al., 2017b).

Thirdly, the stories of employees putting job crafting into practice also highlight some additional benefits. For example, it provides people with a mechanism by which they can genuinely 'bring their whole selves to work' by incorporating their personal strengths, interests and values into the way they do their work. This means incorporating more of who they are into what they do. Similarly, as colleagues learn more about each other's individual differences and preferences, they can allocate work where individuals have the greatest opportunities to contribute and add value. As many of these outcomes have positive implications for organisations as well as the people they employ, there is a case for both employees and organisations to invest their time and effort in job crafting.

8.8 How and When Could Job Crafting Help Me?

In addition to pursuing the benefits previously outlined, we suggest that there are three more circumstances in which job crafting offers distinct advantages.

8.8.1 To Take Control of Your Well-Being

Job crafting can shift the balance of costs and benefits in work and so help safeguard, promote and manage well-being. In general, demands are characteristics of employees' jobs which take energy from them. They include work overload and emotional and physical demands. They constitute the costs side of the ledger. By reducing those elements that drain us of energy or even create stress, as described in Chap. 3, we prevent ill-health or burnout.

Resources are characteristics of the job which give employees energy and include autonomy, feedback and social support. These are the corresponding benefits in the ledger. Job crafting can be used to shift the balance between these two to ensure employees have enough supportive resources to cope with, and even be motivated by, the demands of their jobs.

Problems arise in any walk of life when the costs outweigh the benefits. When employees have insufficient resources to cope with or overcome their demands, their well-being will suffer unless some demands are removed or more resources are provided. Employees can use job crafting in such situations to establish which demands are most costly and practice task crafting to minimise the impact of, or completely remove, these tasks. For example, this could involve seeking to delegate some of the work to a colleague. Alternatively, more resources might be provided such as more team members to reduce workload or more autonomy to carry out the work as the employee chooses.

Job crafting can also be utilised preventatively to protect employee well-being before a problem arises. Employees can use the practice to identify and build in a buffer of resources to protect them from periods of predictable high demand. Relational crafting, for example, could be used to increase social resources in terms of support from a mentoring relationship or a new workplace friend. Task crafting could also be used to decrease potential future hindering demands, for example, by seeking to automate or improve the efficiency of a process-heavy task.

8.8.2 To Support Your Development Throughout Your Career

Job crafting is not a one-off practice; it is a continuous process in which employees make multiple changes over time to shape and mould their work to suit them better. In turn, job crafting can be used by employees to support their development through each of the key transitions that define career progression throughout the employee life cycle.

In the early years of employees' careers, job crafting can be used as a tool to incorporate the new tasks and relationships required to broaden individuals' professional horizons and experiences. Over time, developing employees may wish to use cognitive crafting to reframe administrative tasks increasingly perceived as mundane or routine. At a certain point, task crafting could even be utilised to remove these tasks, and, with increasing autonomy, cognitive crafting may repeatedly be deployed to incorporate an individual's evolving interests, strengths and values in their work.

Mid-career, employees may feel they are stagnating in their role and use task crafting to try out new activities and explore potential areas of interest. Later, employees may feel they have lost sight of their individual meaning, purpose and values and wish to build these into their job, turning their jobs into their passion projects before the end of their career using all three forms of crafting.

8.8.3 To Ease the Transition into Retirement

At the end of a career, crafting can also be used to enable a phased exit from the workplace. As most industrialised countries see the retirement age rise in proportion to ageing populations, people are retiring later than ever. On top of this, employees have increasingly demanding expectations of how much control they have over how and when they retire. These expectations are reflected in the shift seen as fewer engage in the traditional 'cliff-edge' retirement where they stop working entirely from one day to the next. It is becoming more common to seek a phased approach to retirement: a glide slope of reduced time at work that allows a more gradual winding down to retirement.

There is a growing need for strategies and mechanisms which enable 'sustainable employment': the extent to which employees have the capacity and desire to remain working now and in the future. Job crafting provides the mechanism needed for employees to maintain their own sustainable employment; they can use the practice to continually adjust the demands placed on them in a way which matches and manages their changing levels of available energy and other resources.

Specifically, to achieve a sustainable approach, employees may identify the specific job demands causing them to want or need to retire and seek to minimise or remove their detrimental impact. For example, a sales manager may find travel increasingly physically taxing and use relational crafting to swap the method of communication from face-to-face meetings to videoconferences.

8.9 But Wait, I Can't Job Craft!

Can everyone job craft? There are circumstances that make it much more difficult such as an inflexible culture in an organisation, a low level of autonomy at work or high levels of interdependence between roles. Whilst these factors can indeed influence the extent to which there are opportunities for employees to job craft, the good news is that job crafting is itself highly flexible and enables employees to overcome barriers to job crafting. For example, employees need to engage in only one of the three types of crafting to craft, and crafting does not need to take place at a macro-level or team level; it can also include small but significant micro-level changes to an individual's role.

Furthermore, employees in highly rigid and constrained jobs have described a number of ways in which they have job crafted:

- Machine operators on assembly lines required to perform identical tasks repeatedly struggled to change their work, so increased their enjoyment of it by forming new relationships with colleagues they previously did not engage with on the line.
- Call centre staff have reported how the need to follow highly structured scripts restricted their ability to craft. These staff have utilised cognitive crafting to re-focus the way they think about their jobs in terms of the positive impact they have on others. One described keeping a diary in their car so they could reflect on and note three ways they had helped someone that day.
- Debt collectors have also said their job design restrains their ability to craft, referring to the pressurised interactions they have with others daily. They have also been found to use cognitive crafting to reframe the purpose of their role from collecting owed assets to helping people transition out of the cycle of debt.

In other words, whatever else is hindered or prevented, cognitive shifts are always possible.

> **Prompts**
>
> If you still feel that you may struggle to job craft, try considering the following prompts to start thinking about ways in which you could.
>
> - *What aspect of the role initially attracted you to it? What were you excited about? Could you use task, cognitive or relational crafting to re-ignite that feeling?*
> - *Try and remember a really great day at work where something made you feel happy, energised or excited. What happened? Why do you think it made you feel like this? Is there a way to incorporate more of this into your work?*
> - *Which tasks or relationships in your current job weigh you down and drain you? Can you identify what it is about them which means they have that effect on you? Are there ways in which you could minimise or remove the impact these have on you?*
> - *Think about roles you envy others holding, what is it about them that you desire? Can you think of ways you could build this into your existing job?*
> - *What do you see as the overall meaning and purpose of your work? Who is most impacted by what do you do? How does that make you feel?*

8.10 Practical Considerations

When utilised correctly, job crafting provides employees with a way in which they can improve their life, while continuing to add value to organisations through their work. Despite this, there are some key considerations that must be made to ensure job crafting remains a productive and mutually beneficial practice for all.

Primarily, and to the relief of managers, job crafting is not about employees re-designing their roles to the point they no longer deliver results or contribute what the organisation needs. Nor should it promote a dysfunctional work ethic which seeks to disregard or remove all the less glamorous and appealing aspects of work. Rather, job crafting is about finding a way to deliver the original responsibilities, meaning and purpose of the role in a way that is better aligned with employees' strengths, interests and values.

When crafting, employees must consider the interconnected and interdependent nature of roles within organisations because changes made to their roles through crafting are likely to influence others. In addition, the extent to which employees engage in crafting is governed by individual and contextual differences. This means that even members of the same teams are unlikely to all craft to the same extent as one another or in the same ways. Considering these two factors together highlights the need for crafting to be a shared, considerate and transparent activity.

Indeed, research illustrates how inconsiderate crafting can result in colleagues having increased workloads, and more conflict with the job crafters themselves (Dierdorff & Jensen, 2017; Tims et al., 2015). Those engaging in job crafting should keep the dialogue about their crafting activities open with their colleagues and managers. In that way, they can avoid their crafting 'stepping on someone's toes', leaving any tasks uncompleted or causing someone to feel left out.

Crafters should not only consider their colleagues; they should include them! Team-crafting educates colleagues about each other's individual differences and can help employees identify where their colleagues' strengths and interests lie. This can provide opportunities to re-arrange elements for everyone's mutual benefit. Over time, improvements in teams' awareness of each other's individual differences should also enable them to field opportunities for each other.

8.11 Summary and Conclusion

This chapter has introduced the art and science of job crafting. It has highlighted how job crafting is the product of the modern workforce's increasing expectations and demands for autonomy and ownership of their roles. The chapter has also sought to explain what job crafting looks like beyond the academic concept, placing the practice in the world of work and brought to life through multiple examples. The practice itself has been shown to be highly beneficial for employees and employers alike, when practised correctly and considerately. In turn, the practicalities which must be considered when crafting have also been discussed. The concept of job crafting can be transformed into the easy exercise outlined in the next chapter. Read on and map out the blueprint of your current role, and what you want it to look like going forward!

References

Bakker, A. B., Tims, M., & Derks, D. (2012). Proactive personality and job performance: The role of job crafting and work engagement. *Human Relations, 65*, 1359–1378.

Berg, J. M., Dutton, J. E., & Wrzesniewski, A. (2008). What is job crafting and why does it matter. Retrieved form the website of Positive Organizational Scholarship on December 23, 2020.

Dierdorff, E. C., & Jensen, J. M. (2017). Crafting in context: Exploring when job crafting is dysfunctional for performance effectiveness. *Journal of Applied Psychology, 103*, 463–477.

Dutton, J. E., Debebe, G., & Wrzesniewski, A. (2016). Being valued and devalued at work: A social valuing perspective. In *Qualitative organizational research: Best papers from the Davis Conference on Qualitative Research, 3*, 9–52. Information Age.

Ghitulescu, B. E. (2007). Shaping tasks and relationships at work: Examining the antecedents and consequences of employee job crafting (Doctoral dissertation, University of Pittsburgh, America). http://d-scholarship.pitt.edu/10312/1/ghitulescube_etd.pdf

Gordon, H. J., Demerouti, E., Le Blanc, P. M., Bakker, A. B., Bipp, T., & Verhagen, M. A. (2018). Individual job redesign: Job crafting interventions in healthcare. *Journal of Vocational Behavior, 104*, 98–114.

Leana, C., Appelbaum, E., & Shevchuk, I. (2009). Work process and quality of care in early childhood education: The role of job crafting. *Academy of Management Journal, 52*, 1169–1192.

Pendleton, D., & Furnham, A. F. (2016). *Leadership: All you need to know* (2nd ed.). Palgrave Macmillan.

Pendleton, D., Furnham, A., & Cowell, C. (2021). *Leadership: No more heroes* (3rd ed.). Palgrave Macmillan.

Tims, M., & Bakker, A. B. (2010). Job crafting: Towards a new model of individual job redesign. *SA Journal of Industrial Psychology, 36*(2), 1–9.

Tims, M., Bakker, A. B., & Derks, D. (2015). Job crafting and job performance: A longitudinal study. *European Journal of Work and Organizational Psychology, 24*, 914–928.

Van den Heuvel, M., Demerouti, E., & Peeters, M. C. (2015). The job crafting intervention: Effects on job resources, self-efficacy, and affective well-being. *Journal of Occupational and Organizational Psychology, 88*, 511–532.

Van Wingerden, J., Bakker, A. B., & Derks, D. (2017a). The longitudinal impact of a job crafting intervention. *European Journal of Work and Organizational Psychology, 26*, 107–119.

Van Wingerden, J., Bakker, A. B., & Derks, D. (2017b). Fostering employee well-being via a job crafting intervention. *Journal of Vocational Behavior, 100*, 164–174.

Van Wingerden, J., & Poell, R. F. (2017). Employees POC and in role performance: The mediating role of job crafting and work engagement. *Frontiers in Psychology, 8*, article 1876.

Wrzesniewski, A., & Dutton, J. E. (2001). Crafting a job: Revisioning employees as active crafters of their work. *Academy of Management Review, 26*(2), 179–201.

Wrzesniewski, A., Dutton, J., & Debebe, G. (2003). Interpersonal sensemaking and the meaning of work. *Research in Organizational Behavior, 25*, 93–135. https://doi.org/10.1016/S0191-3085(03)25003-6

9

Leadership in the Fourth Industrial Age

Leaders can create the conditions in which people become more engaged in their work and make positive suggestions about how it could be changed for the better. Involving, democratised leadership suits the twenty-first century well and is consistent with its place in history.

It has been argued that we are now living and working in the fourth industrial age. The first industrial revolution was created by the steam engine that broke the link between animal effort (men, horses, oxen and the like) and effect, bringing on the mechanisation revolution. It was so transformative that it has been dubbed THE industrial revolution that heralded THE industrial age. Industries were created and industrialisation enabled such extensive change that world orders were overturned. The nations that industrialised first or early stole a march on those that were slower to transform in this way. The British Empire, for example, accelerated around the globe propelled by steam power.

The second revolution was that of mass production and electricity. It changed the economics of manufacturing and made products available on a scale unimagined in earlier ages. The third revolution captured the potential of computers and computing in an age of digitisation, systems and automation. It was claimed, contentiously, that Thomas Watson,

President of IBM, predicted in 1943 that there may be a world market for five computers, and Ken Olsen, President of DEC, had argued in 1977 that there was no reason why anybody would want a computer in their homes. However, the third industrial revolution led to such a proliferation of personal and mobile computers that there are very few homes in the wealthier countries that do not have access to several personal or mobile computers, all of which had many times the computing power of the computers on the spacecraft that first took man to the moon.[1]

The fourth industrial revolution (4IR) has been created around new technologies with extraordinary impact and scope including artificial intelligence, genome editing, augmented reality, robotics and 3-D printing. Yet it is the convergence of digital, biological and physical innovations that seems to expand their potential exponentially according to Klaus Schwab, Founder and Executive Chairman of the World Economic Forum.

The still-unrealised potential of 4IR is huge, for both 'good' and 'bad', although perhaps it is simplistic to apply such value-laden terms here. It could bring in an age of increasing leisure, prosperity, education and enlightenment, a new golden age of exploration, or an age of massive inequalities and conflict brought about by competition for resources and the disruption of markets around the globe as automation substitutes for labour. The outcome, Schwab argues, is up to us and how we make choices along the way. It is possible that 'the displacement of workers by technology will, in aggregate, result in a net increase in safe and rewarding jobs' (Schwab, 2016). On balance, Schwab argues, 4IR is not so much a prediction as a call to action to make our shared future both inclusive and human-centred so that we can, presumably, reap the benefits rather than the whirlwind. Human-centred AI would shape its purpose to enhance rather than threaten human existence, taking account of economic and moral issues.

We are emerging into a new world of bewildering change, choices and possibilities.

---

[1] Ian Goldin and Robert Muggah in *Terra Incognita* (2020) estimate that our smartphones in 2020 now have '100,000 times the processing power and 7 million times the memory' of the computers that guided Apollo 11 to the moon in 1969.

- Whereas it has always been difficult to predict the future with any certainty, now it is impossible to find any brief period of stability in which to analyse the options. They have to be analysed on the fly.
- Whereas, in the 1980s, the term VUCA was coined to remind us all of the volatility, uncertainty, complexity and ambiguity that bedevilled planning, now it is hard to establish and agree on even the parameters of a problem that needs to be addressed. Sheer pace and unpredictability can force radical actions to be implemented that have not hitherto been considered.
- Whereas many of the concerns and priorities of nations were reasonably well understood and moved at a rapid but manageable pace, now they have been hit by a tidal wave of disruption and by the clash of health-related and economic preoccupations. The coronavirus pandemic of 2020 is a powerful illustration moving from a generic, low-likelihood, vague possibility to a local, remote outbreak, into a global health and economic disaster in a few short months.

Cue leadership! Steady states can be administered effectively. Change, disruption and crisis call for leadership. In 4IR, leadership needs to tackle a bewildering array of issues simultaneously. It also needs to anticipate the interconnected nature of the society in which we all now live so that we do not solve one problem only to cause another. None of this is easy, but there are principles to guide us as we navigate our future together.

The theme of this book is change at work and in the home. We have raised the possibility that each of us may be able to analyse, rethink and change our experience of both home and work using job crafting techniques. *We want to stress that, since we are now living through times of widespread disruption in our nations and communities, the shackles that have typically held the status quo in place have been weakened if not shattered in all manner of contexts. Change is thus enabled on a broad front including both at work and in the home.* The key questions become: in what directions do we want to provoke change and how might we go about it? So, this chapter considers the issue of leadership.

9.1 Leadership

Many of the current ideas about leadership had their origins in earlier times and in previous industrial ages. Similarly, many approaches to leadership have imagined exceptional individuals in leadership positions making decisions and then seeking to take others with them by building consensus. A relevant exception is the Primary Colours®[2] Approach to Leadership (Pendleton & Furnham, 2012, 2016; Pendleton et al., 2021). Their approach defines the purpose of leadership as '*to create the conditions for people to thrive, individually and collectively, and achieve significant goals*'.

The Primary Colours Approach to Leadership is based on four propositions:

1. The 'Primary Colours Model' describes the territory of leadership and answers the question: what do leaders have to do? It suggests seven tasks across three domains that create the conditions for success. (See Fig. 9.1 below)
2. It is extremely hard for any individual to excel in all the tasks and to be a complete leader alone.
3. Leaders possess different kinds of strengths and limitations, some of which can readily be changed and others that are more resistant to change.
4. Complete leadership is most likely to come from teams of leaders made up of complementary differences.

This approach to leadership has also been extended to embrace the challenges of leading over longer timescales. Organisations have always needed to develop their people and innovate but, when more fundamental change is called for, there arises a radical challenge to reinvent the organisation more fundamentally. In this context, innovation and the development of people and culture are greater in scope and urgency in order to make the new paradigm or business model work.

---

[2] Primary Colours is a registered trademark of the Edgecumbe Consulting Group Ltd.

9 Leadership in the Fourth Industrial Age

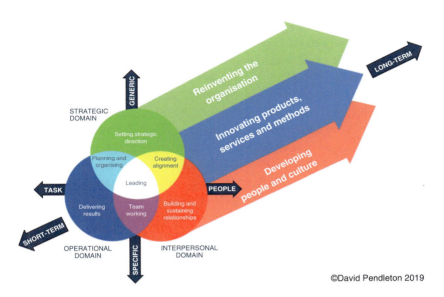

Fig. 9.1 Leadership through time

Reinventing the workplace in the face of new technologies occurs relatively frequently. For example, Fleet Street in London is unrecognisable since mobile computing and new printing technologies rendered old print rooms anachronistic. The continuing growth of social media might yet render newsprint entirely redundant as a means of staying abreast of current affairs, though print may still prove to be immortal. Reinventing the workplace can also happen reactively as a response to change that is mandated, such as in the face of new legislation and social mores. Smoking in the office, male-only top teams, sexist dress codes and a host of other issues have been addressed by changes in the law.

Other significant changes are created proactively by vision and creativity. Freedom to work from home, leisure areas on the office floor, coffee shops at work, crèches in the office or factory are no longer remarkable. They were created in response to new demands and expectations from a more vocal workforce that had choices about where to work in prosperous economic times at the end of the twentieth century and the start of the twenty-first century. Now, despite the recession of 2008 and the pandemic and recession of 2020, new opportunities to reinvent the workplace are upon us and we have to choose how we will respond. More precisely, those of us who lead teams and organisations have the chance to lead this change rather than wait for others to do so.

Job crafting has arrived in some workplaces and is likely to come to a host of others. Leadership, anticipating and embracing this opportunity, can facilitate an organisation moving into the vanguard of change or hold it back. Those who want to be agents of this change will need to understand how to operate the levers of leadership to bring about the changes they seek. In the context of job crafting, essentially a bottom-up activity, leaders do not have to make job crafting happen but rather, as we have argued, create the right conditions, making it safe and easy. Encouragement and removing the obstacles may be all that is needed.

9.1.1 The Territory of Leadership: What Do Leaders Have to Do?

The latest version of the Primary Colours Model of Leadership shows the longer-term tasks. It appears here as Fig. 9.1 (Pendleton et al., 2021). It describes the tasks that leaders need to achieve or ensure are achieved by others. The tasks are arranged in domains: strategic, operational and inter-personal.

- The *strategic* domain is focused on the future in both the shorter and longer terms. In VUCA terms, it is the domain where there is maximum uncertainty and unpredictability.
- The *operational* domain is focused on the present and is much more certain. It is filled with facts, schedules and details, targets, plans and contingencies. It is the domain where there is a great deal of complexity.
- The *inter-personal* domain is focused on the people in the organisation, and deals with relationships, alignment and commitment, values, beliefs and culture. It is the domain where a great deal of ambiguity is encountered. Having to work in all three domains simultaneously makes leadership challenging.

The specific leadership tasks are also important to understand. Here we can relate them to the challenge of creating an organisation that has a culture to foster job crafting and bottom-up decision-making, giving everyone a voice at work.

9.1.2 The Leadership Tasks

1. **Setting strategic direction**. This task sits uniquely in the strategic domain and includes many other elements associated with high-level leadership. It begins, not by looking inside the organisation, but around it to understand what is happening in the world that may have profound implications for the organisation's future. This is horizon scanning. Sense has to be made of the market, and the economic, social and technical environment. This is an active process, perhaps better described as <u>creating</u> the story to which the organisation has to respond. When Steve Jobs noticed the convergence of digital technologies, he created a narrative of how these could fit into emerging lifestyles in a way that nobody else had so clearly articulated. He recognised the implications for Apple and set off to create a suite of products based on cool design, attractive and intuitive user interfaces and very high-quality manufacture. Sense-making made possible the identification of a vision and strategy to orient the organisation to its best future.

   Elements of this process are vague and ill-defined at the start. To illustrate this point, David Pendleton et al. (2021) tell the story of Tony Tyler who became Director-General of IATA, the International Air Transport Association in 2011. He soon discovered that the organisation had an urgent need for a new strategy to galvanise its people and align their efforts. He had spent almost his entire career in the airline industry and knew its requirements from personal experience. The industry was relatively safe and secure but needed to become much more sustainable: more profitable. He posed this conundrum to the senior managers in IATA in a vision statement which proposed that IATA had to become a source of innovation and change in the industry to serve their clear and shared goal of helping create an industry that was safe, secure *and profitable*. This became the start of a strategy defining process that involved a large number of people in the organisation.

From a clear strategic direction, the foundation of a strategy may be constructed. It cannot remain vague, though it inevitably starts this way. Purpose, Vision, Mission and Values all need to be defined along with strategy itself: the plan to which the organisation will align and that will help it identify the must-win battles, the priorities, the choices and hence also the activities that have to stop in order not to de-focus effort.

A critical megatrend in the organisational and social landscape now is the increasing expectation of millennials and others to have a voice at work. The old psychological contract of a job for life in exchange for employee compliance is dead and has been for some time. All organisations in the twenty-first century need to figure out how they will involve their people in decision-making. Now, as leaders set strategic direction, they need to incorporate dialogue and consultation into their thinking about organisational culture so that bottom-up initiatives are fostered in the service of the organisation's purpose, vision, mission and strategy. This then becomes the context into which the bottom-up initiative of job crafting fits and feels normal.

2. **Creating alignment**

Alignment of the electrons is the difference between a 40-watt lightbulb that can barely light a closet and a 40-watt laser that can punch holes in steel. Analogously, in organisations, alignment of people with the purpose, values and strategy of an organisation liberates and magnifies their energy and contributions. Alignment cannot be demanded; it is the gift of those who feel committed to the organisation and are invested in wanting it to succeed. It is typically given by those who feel proud of the organisation's purpose, who feel a part of it, who are enthusiastic about how the organisation operates and who subscribe to its values.

Alignment can be aided by making people feel welcome in the organisation, giving them a voice to be heard and a role in planning and organising the execution of the organisation's activities. It can be reduced or destroyed by demanding compliance without involvement, by hypocrisy (saying one thing and doing another) or by simply lying. There is nothing complex about this but these principles are not as common as they could be. Activities that do harm to alignment also reduce energy and effort at work. Physicists, on the one hand, cite the law of conservation of energy which states that energy can be neither created nor destroyed; it can only be transferred or transformed from one form to another. Psychologists, on the other hand, know very well that human energy can be created and enhanced, reduced or destroyed.

In the context of the workplace, any actions that reduce alignment drain us and those that increase alignment create that 'buzz' that sustains the joy of work and its power to re-energise us. Leadership can have a direct impact on alignment.

3. **Planning and organising**

There is a cascade of aims, goals, targets and plans in most organisations ranging across timescales and from macro to micro in scope. Organisations also vary in terms of their environments and markets where a key variable is predictability. Public health organisations, in particular, are painfully aware that what can be predicted in outline may not be predictable in detail. The coronavirus pandemic of 2020 was predicted in outline inasmuch as some kind of pandemic is always a possibility and, in the longer-term, an inevitability: but when might that occur? In the case of coronavirus, the timing and the specific nature of the pandemic was completely impossible to predict, and most of the advanced pandemic planning was erroneously based on the assumption that it would be some kind of flu, which it was not. Volcanologists share the same frustration that the eruptions they can predict in outline are hard to predict with precision.

In the context of creating workplaces that nurture and sustain people, their energy, health and happiness, unpredictability causes distress but cannot be prevented. Accordingly, it is unlikely to cause people to become angry about their employers, since nobody can anticipate that which is genuinely unpredictable. These are the black swan events so often seen as disasters when they are serious and laughed off as Murphy's law when they are trivial. But people feel rightly aggrieved when that which IS predictable is not predicted and that which is able to be anticipated is not planned for. That smacks of either incompetence or negligence.

In the case of the UK government and coronavirus, they ran an exercise in 2016, called *Cygnus*, to help them prepare for a pandemic but then they failed to implement the lessons learned, failing, among other things, to purchase and stockpile sufficient quantities of personal protective equipment, according to Richard Horton, editor of the Lancet in his excellent 2020 book *The Covid-19 Catastrophe: What's Gone Wrong and How to Stop It Happening Again*.

This is somewhat controversial, however. In *Uncharted*, Margaret Heffernan asserts that planning and reality never coincide and the implication is clear: there is little point in planning in any great detail. She implies that it is better to remain vigilant and open to respond rapidly to environmental changes that happen: to strive to be agile. While we agree that a great deal of change is unpredictable, we argue differently in two respects. First, that short-term planning is perfectly feasible, even necessary, to keep an organisation coordinated and its people clear about what is expected of them. Second, that high-level planning helps to think through a number of possible scenarios and develop options. In this way, high-level planning aids agility and does not have to result in detailed plans which then need to be abandoned.

If we are trying, as leaders, to create workplaces in which people thrive, then oversights have to be removed through capable planning and organisation. If not, colleagues may be forgiven for believing that the seniors in the organisation do not care, whatever it may say on their formal statement of organisational values. Values are inferred from what people do, not from what they say and, in the event that words and actions lead to opposite conclusions, then actions speak more convincingly than words.

We must plan and organise well in order to convince our colleagues that we care but we must also involve our colleagues as far as possible in the planning and organisation for several reasons. First, they will become more committed to plans which they have had a role in creating. Second, people closer to the action will be able to put together more effective plans than seniors who are more distant. Third, colleagues who believe they are trusted to make plans will also feel more able to change them if the plans start to unravel. Involvement increases commitment AND alignment.

4. **Building and sustaining relationships**
Ultimately, all organisations are built on the people who run them and serve their purposes. Service organisations have always claimed that they are people-based and they have often proclaimed that 'people are our most important asset'. When this is truly believed and demonstrated, those organisations engender loyalty and commitment. Others deploy this claim as a catch-phrase only to abandon the people when times are hard. They sow the seeds of cynicism in the gap between rhetoric and reality.

Organisations that build authentic relationships create one of the critical elements for success. When deals are negotiated, the best and most lasting agreements suit and benefit all parties. For relationships to be built effectively, all parties have to buy-in to them. Colleagues share experiences and challenges of all kinds. These tend to bind them together unless trust is poor. Customers and suppliers also need to be treated well if they are to respond with their loyalty. Even the communities in which organisations are based expect to be treated with a measure of care and respect. Relationship building is a key element of building and leading an organisation that will last.

In the context of job crafting, we advocate building a culture in which all parties recognise the legitimacy of the needs of others. This is an ethical, caring culture. There is no room for cynicism here. Commercial organisations have to pay attention minimally to the needs of colleagues, customers, shareholders and their local communities. If they do not, any of these groups can do the organisation harm. But it is not necessary to be defensive about this. A virtuous circle can be created if there is openness, honesty and trust in the relationships.

The point here about leadership is that many organisations take their lead from those who are most senior and those who have been around the longest. They set the tone by setting the example they want to be followed. All this can stem from the values of certain key players. But in the context of a twenty-first-century organisation, democratisation of decision-making and increasing sensitivity are becoming the norm, abandoning or at least de-emphasising the macho competitiveness of the former century. Pendleton et al. (2021) emphasised this point by showing how the personality attribute of Agreeableness (including trust, altruism and compassion) is becoming a more powerful predictor of leadership effectiveness than Extraversion (including assertiveness and pace).

The culture that builds and sustains relationships with all stakeholders suits well the requirements for job crafting and for building workplaces that are salutogenic rather than pathogenic: that promote well-being rather than strain and ill-health.

5. **Team working**

How does a group differ from a team? Teams serve common purposes and work inter-dependently. This requires a level of maturity that transcends the assertion of independence. Effective teams operate synergistically: they can achieve more together than the sum of the parts. Ineffective teams do the precise opposite: they get in each other's way and become less than the sum of the parts. This is obvious and well-known but less well-known, and less common, may be the role of teams in creating resilience and adaptation. Gallup asserts the power of having a 'best friend' at work, and this has become one of Gallup's 12 key survey questions. We assert that teams have a further role in creativity and support. Michael West and colleagues have demonstrated, for example, that, in the most effective healthcare teams, there is greater employee satisfaction, innovation and even better mental health (Borrill and West 2002). It is a task of leadership to ensure that teams work well to achieve their goals.

Job crafting, as we have seen in earlier chapters, is one means of helping a team to thrive since it will involve putting all key tasks on the table for the team to discuss and allocate in the most effective way. Minimally, it should be possible to ensure that no individual is permanently stuck with the drudgery of uninteresting, stressful and thankless work. Realistically, it should be possible to ensure that each team member's portfolio of tasks is a good mix so that they willingly take the rough with the smooth. Ideally, it may be possible to both automate those tasks that nobody enjoys and allocate to individuals tasks that they love.

How close it is possible to get to the ideal is a matter of the team's ingenuity. But the team members need to be assured that it is safe for them to analyse their work in this way. Leaders who are genuinely motivated to do their best for their people will find themselves drawn to those actions that make teams more effective since they benefit both the team members and the organisation as a whole. Certainly, an ineffective team is a wasted resource and in need of attention.

6. **Delivering results**
It is a truism that delivering results matters and, for many, it would go without saying. But the real issue is not how to deliver results so much as how to *sustain* the delivery of results over time. Short-term delivery would be counter-productive if the effort to deliver hindered or prevented the delivery of results in the medium or longer term. In the face of a crisis, the issue of sustainability will often be set aside briefly but, at all other times, it is crucial.

This book advocates employee involvement in decision-making, and especially with respect to job crafting, as one way in which the sustainability of results may be addressed. Few people are likely to give of their best if their work is unstimulating, relentless and stressful. But what may stimulate one person may bore another. What one person finds relentless or stressful may suit another very well. The opportunity, therefore, to take part in the audit and review that is job crafting makes it possible to ensure that the work allocated to each team member is as good a fit as the work allows. It also has the potential to provoke serious innovation to transform what is done and the way it is achieved so that everyone benefits.

Leaders interested in the sustained achievement of results need to create a workplace in which colleagues are fully engaged, not merely compliant. Leadership that encourages participation in continually seeking ways to improve how things are done serves the interest of all stakeholders.

7. **Leading**
Leading has two principal functions: to choose and to sustain. It chooses the focus of the team or organisation for a time: choosing among the other leadership tasks. It also chooses who is best to lead during that phase since leaders are more skilled and better suited to

leading in some of the leadership tasks rather than others. Yet it also sustains effort when it is at risk of flagging.

Choosing the focus of the team involves appreciating the ways in which the context is varying, its demands and pressures. It also involves monitoring how well the organisation is performing and recommends shifts in focus as required. In terms of the primary colours approach to leadership, issues may arise in any of the three domains (strategic, operational, interpersonal), singly or in combination and each may require a different response. Yet, if the culture has facilitated the use of job crafting and its involving processes, then insights may be gathered from most parts of the organisation, more brains can be directed to analysing the issues and more hands can be directed to solving the problems. This is the power of engagement and of demonstrating trust in the intelligence of colleagues. It makes the investment in them and in the culture worthwhile.

The task of Leading is well illustrated by the orchestral conductor. He or she does not make a sound, yet by respecting, recognising and deploying the differences between individuals they bring out the best in the individuals and the orchestra as a whole while remaining faithful to the music as created by the composer. Similarly, leaders can orchestrate their teams in a way which enables each to craft to their strengths, values, interests and personality ensuring this is conducted in a way that ensures individual actions are collectively aligned with the organisational strategy and objectives.

8. **In the longer term**

Leadership in the longer-term draws attention to three major tasks:

- Reinventing the organisation
- Innovating systems, products and services
- Developing people and culture

In these tasks, there is a hidden assumption. Each organisation is built around a current, implicit operating model and there exists in parallel a host of future possible models. Currently, the organisation will have a more or less explicit purpose, vision, mission and strategy. If it is a commercial organisation, it will have its current business model. Within this current 'version' of itself, there is a constant need to innovate (in order to compete) and to develop the people and culture (in order to sustain motivation and capability). But, from time to time, there is a need or an opportunity to rethink, re-imagine and reinvent the organisation as a whole. At these times, the innovation and development agendas take on a far greater importance.

To illustrate these points, consider the story of Menzies. Their journey demonstrates continuous innovation and development built around infrequent, radical transformations that reinvented their organisation. Founded in 1833, John Menzies (now PLC) was a start-up retailer with a single shop in Princes Street in Edinburgh. It sold newspapers to the public. As time progressed, the company expanded its retail operations to more shops in Scotland and then in England. As rail transport expanded, Menzies moved increasingly into wholesale distribution, still using horse-drawn vehicles until it acquired its first motorised vehicle in 1910. The next decade saw them fully motorise their fleet and, in the second half of the twentieth century, Menzies were at the cutting edge of using computer systems to help manage distribution. They moved increasingly into transportation and specifically air transport, courier services and cargo, acquiring businesses along the way consistent with their new direction.

On their journey, Menzies went into the toy business, Early Learning Centre, games and the like but a sea change happened in 1998 when they sold their retail business to WH Smith to focus entirely on aviation. They now describe themselves in the history section of their website as a 'pure-play aviation business'. They had started in retailing before computers and aircraft existed but they moved with the times and opportunities to emerge as an aviation business.

Within each business model, they innovated and acquired in order to grow. The development agenda must have been considerable along the way and those who worked in the organisation over longer timescales would have experienced a rich series of transformations.

The Danaher Corporation is another case in point. Danaher may be the most successful organisation that many people have never heard of. Inspection of their share price over time demonstrates how extraordinary has been their growth. Named after a swift-flowing river in Montana, the company has embodied nimble and rapid innovation based on continuous improvement. Today they have more than 20 operating companies and 59,000 employees serving a purpose: to help realise life's potential. They pride themselves in adapting quickly to changes in business and technology using continuous improvement and customer satisfaction as their guiding principles.

Success at Danaher is achieved through the Danaher Business System (DBS) which embodies their guiding principles. It is a well-documented process that leaves little to chance. They acquire businesses that will benefit from the DBS and train the employees of each business they acquire in how to operate the DBS.

At Danaher, they help organisations rethink their businesses, innovate their methods and develop their people so that the entire system is coherent and self-sustaining. They make change a way of life, and their story and methods form one of the most impressive cases taught at Harvard Business School.

9.2 Summary and Conclusion

Gardeners know the power of getting the conditions right for growth. They will invest time, effort and money in getting the soil right to grow their chosen crops within the climate conditions in which their garden sits. Leadership has a similar focus on getting the conditions right for success. Good people hired with enthusiasm and developed into their roles will contribute well. But, if those roles do not evolve and grow with them, even committed employees will lose enthusiasm and start to underperform. Wise leaders will go to considerable lengths to avoid the need to write that apocryphal testimonial *'he left us as he joined us, fired with enthusiasm'*.

All of us change over time: our needs, aspirations, attitudes and the like. Some of these changes are unique to each individual, whereas others, as we demonstrated in Chap. 4, follow a somewhat more predictable pattern as the seasons of our lives change. Leaders who are determined to pursue the right conditions for people and organisations to thrive, do not need to speculate or guess what these changing needs will be or how they will manifest themselves. They can create a culture in which their people have a voice that is welcomed and can make job crafting safe and easy, even enabling it to take root in their organisations.

The alternative is to create the conditions for the traditional approach to work-life balance where people have to escape the workplace in order to recharge their batteries. We are proposing that it is preferable to create workplaces that are more self-sustaining, in which the mix of tasks and the overall experience of work each day replenishes the energy used in some aspects of the work by the re-energising effects of other aspects of the work. When a colleague returns home from this kind of workplace, he or she is in good shape to contribute to the well-being of the family or to enjoy their personal life to the fullest extent rather than having to enter a rapid recovery phase before work recommences.

References

Borrill, C., & West, M. (2002). Team working and effectiveness in health care: findings from the healthcare team effectiveness project. Birmingham. Aston Centre for Health Service Organisation Research.

Pendleton, D., & Furnham, F. (2012). *Leadership: All you need to know*. Palgrave Macmillan.

Pendleton, D., & Furnham, F. (2016). *Leadership: All you need to know*. Palgrave Macmillan.

Pendleton, D., Furnham, F., & Cowell, J. (2021). *Leadership: No more heroes*. Palgrave Macmillan.

Schwab, K. (2016). *The fourth industrial revolution: What it means, how to respond*. World Economic Forum.

10

Enabling Job Crafting, a Call to Action

The previous chapter focused on leadership but leaders are not the only actors who can foster the right context and culture for job crafting. Here we consider a broader range of actions and actors. Job crafting is a 'unicorn' practice: highly appealing but rare since it has yet to become widely adopted across organisations. The appeal comes from its refreshing ability to provide employees with the empowerment and ownership they crave to shape the content of their work and their experience of it. However, it also presents a challenge since employees cannot be made to job craft. Job crafting has emerged as an employee-initiated process. It is not something that is best implemented top-down. Just as pastry chefs cannot force their baked goods to rise but can carefully create the conditions they know promote rising, bosses cannot mandate the confidence and enthusiasm that leads to job crafting, but they can carefully create the conditions they know to enable it.

This chapter will describe the conditions research has found make job crafting more likely. We will then take you through our 'playbook' of interventions, exercises and activities derived from the research on job crafting and our own consulting experience working with clients.

10.1 Making Job Crafting More Likely

The starting point is quite basic. There are two key ingredients for crafting: perception and capability. Employees must first recognise opportunities for change in their role (known in the research as 'perceived opportunities' to craft) and they must believe they personally have the capability to make those changes (known in the research as 'job crafting self-efficacy' or JCSE).

> *Job crafting self-efficacy is a person's beliefs about his or her own capability to modify demands and resources present at their job to better fit their needs and preferences.* (Roczniewska et al., 2020)

The suggestions in this playbook have been designed to enhance both perceived opportunities to craft and also employees' job crafting self-efficacy.

10.1.1 The Power of Perception

To start with the fundamentals, before employees engage in job crafting, they must perceive opportunities to do so. This logical relationship has been repeatedly confirmed by both qualitative and quantitative research (Van Wingerden et al., 2013, 2018). One study used a simple diary exercise which demonstrated that participants who successfully job crafted explicitly reported that the perception of an opportunity to craft came first. Similarly, those who did not craft cited a lack of perceived opportunities as the reason. So, influencing how these matters are perceived is far from incidental.

Chloe Hodgkinson's research (2018) established the conditions required for employees to perceive opportunities to craft. Interviews were conducted with employees exploring the organisational characteristics which influenced the extent to which they perceived opportunities to, and did, job craft. These findings have been translated into the following four-step framework for creating the conditions for crafting:

1. Make sure employees know that they have *permission* to job craft.
2. Create a culture where employees feel *psychologically safe* to experiment and take risks.
3. Give employees the *control* they need to craft through trust and autonomy.
4. Ensure employees have the *capacity* to craft by promoting realistic workloads, clear role boundaries and protected crafting time.

10.1.2   Creating Opportunities

It is vital that employees are empowered to adapt their job descriptions and responsibilities, thus creating work that is personally meaningful, engaging and satisfying to them. This does not entail changing the job description *per se*, but it involves creating the freedom to choose *how* the work is done: the means to the end. Those seeking to enable job crafting in employees must also create and promote *opportunities* to do so. To expand on the four steps outlined above:

1. *Permission*

   Ensure employees know they have permission to craft at every level; top-down permission from the organisation and management and horizontally from colleagues, peers and team members. Permission is best communicated explicitly by leaders, managers and colleagues, and illustrated implicitly through organisational culture and processes that enable crafting, embedding it throughout the organization. Once established as a common practice, it feeds into a culture that implicitly grants others permission to craft.

2. *Psychological Safety*

   Job crafting involves the exploration, adaptation and pursuit of new and existing ideas, activities, relationships and ways of thinking without provoking disapproval from those loyal to the *status quo*. If we want employees to engage in such pursuits, it is crucial to create a culture of psychological safety.

According to Amy Edmondson, a leading American leadership scholar, psychological safety describes *'perceptions of the consequences of taking interpersonal risks in a particular context such as a workplace.'* Psychologically safe team members *'feel confident that no one on the team will embarrass or punish anyone else for admitting a mistake, asking a question, or offering a new idea'* (Edmondson, 2018). Clearly, this includes the general matter of suggesting that how we do things can, and should, change (see Table 10.1).

Psychologically safe environments are conducive to comfort with change and acknowledge that it inevitably brings potential risks and errors. Psychologically safe environments are likely to feature open dialogue and feedback, giving employees confidence that they can share innovative crafting ideas, experiment with new job crafting goals and make mistakes in the process without fear of being judged or scrutinised. Indeed, mistakes and risk-taking in such environments are not perceived as failure or negligence, but as evidence of an innovative mindset, learning, experimentation and growth.

Table 10.1 Amy Edmondson's safety survey (Edmondson, 2018)

Do you feel psychologically safe in your team? Use this measure, created for Google by Amy Edmondson, to do a quick audit:
To what extent do you agree or disagree with the following statements?
Item
If you make a mistake on this team, it is often held against you.
Members of this team are able to bring up problems and tough issues.
People on this team sometimes reject others for being different.
It is safe to take a risk on this team.
It is difficult to ask other members of this team for help.
No one on this team would deliberately act in a way that undermines my efforts.
Working with members of this team, my unique skills and talents are valued and utilised.
The balance between the amount of positive or negative responses will give you an indication of whether your team is psychologically safe or not. It will also suggest what you may need to work on to increase the feeling of safety.

3. *Control*

A key aspect of job crafting is choice over how our work is designed and tailored to us. Employees need to have sufficient control over their working life to feel able to experiment with job crafting. They need to feel they are trusted and have a measure of autonomy to make decisions about their work. The benefits of granting employees control extend beyond job crafting. In the twenty-first century workplace, greater autonomy is the antidote to micromanagement that saps most people of enthusiasm and commitment.

4. *Capacity*

From an emotional point of view, the analytical and creative thinking job crafting requires demands sufficient energy to be invested in it. From a practical point of view, employees need sufficient time to consider and conduct crafting activities. Both emotional and practical considerations are heavily influenced by the extent to which employees have manageable workloads which offer the flexibility to engage in crafting. Allowing employees to designate protected time to develop, pursue interests, innovate and craft is crucial but not easy in a busy workplace.

Further, employees' understanding of their roles is key to ensuring they feel able to experiment. Employees need role clarity, an understanding of what is expected of them, what the boundaries of their roles are (and whether they are safe to operate outside of these) and also the extent to which their role is interdependent on others.

10.2 Creating Opportunities Throughout the Organisation

Many different groups can influence employees' job crafting. In the following sections, we will break these down into actions for the leadership team, Human Resources, Occupational Health, line managers and teams. These groups include some of the most powerful sources of influence in organisations.

10.2.1 The Leadership Team

There are two key responsibilities for those charged with leading the organisation, in the context of job crafting and the promotion of all innovative thinking and actions. These are creating a culture that makes crafting safe (permission and psychological safety) and easy (control and capacity).

1. *Practice and Champion Job Crafting*

The leadership team should job craft themselves. Tailoring their work to themselves as individuals will generate buy-in to the practice. Further, publicly doing so will model crafting behaviours to others, and inspire employees to craft themselves.

2. *Talk About It*

The more we talk about it, the more we bring job crafting into the mainstream culture of the organisation. Telling illustrative stories about job crafting and the impact it has sends the right signals to employees throughout the organisation.

3. *Allow Flexible Working*

Flexible working facilitates job crafting. It grants employees the chance to reconfigure how they approach their work and home lives in a way which makes it a balance, not a battle between the two. In this way, individuals can explore how commitment to both home and work can more easily co-exist and even become synergistic. But individuals have to do this for themselves since only they know how the expectations of the actors in each setting can be met.

The force of this matter is not to be underestimated. We are witnessing a shift in employee expectations towards those of a consumer. They expect flexibility and well-being as standard, whilst organisations are finding it increasingly hard to attract and retain talent. Job shortages after recessions tend to be temporary. By promoting flexible working options for employees to design the working patterns that best suit them, the needs of both the organisation and employees can be met. These include condensed workweeks, job sharing, remote working and customised working hours.

This trend has been growing slowly for several decades and has been accelerated by the experience of working through the coronavirus pandemic. Widespread migration to working from home during lockdown highlighted to many that conflating work and the workplace was outdated and unnecessary. Moving forward, organisations need to think about how they can capitalise on the lessons that the pandemic has gifted us. It should not be a case of one or the other, work or home, it's about finding the mix which best suits each employee. A focus on *what* needs to be done rather than *how* it is done makes this easier. In fact, there is even an initiative to do away with job descriptions entirely since they create a package deal with inflexible, fixed boundaries. These can be replaced by aggregated lists of tasks to be completed and which can be repackaged many times to suit the needs of teams according to a new book by Ravin Jesuthasan and John Boudreau published by MIT Press in 2021.

10.2.2 Human Resources

Human Resources (HR) is the function that determines how any employee interacts with the organisation, its systems and processes within the bounds of employment law. It is the function, typically, that measures the state of the workforce: its morale, satisfaction and engagement and enables the organisation through employee and management development.

1. *Tracking and Measuring*

   Deploying surveys and tracking data on absenteeism, employee turnover, vacancy rates and the like, HR detects how the organisation's culture and climate are functioning and their impact on the folk who work in the organisation. These matters are relevant for enabling job crafting in several ways. First, they can gauge whether key messages have been received and understood. Unless permission to engage in job crafting is heard, understood and trusted, it will not happen. Second, HR can ascertain whether employees feel sufficiently empowered to make suggestions and changes to how they work. Third, they can estimate the extent to which opportunities to engage in job crafting are being taken and whether they are having a positive impact on climate and engagement. This is a tracking function.

2. Learning and Development

HR also typically manages the learning and development function (L&D). Development programmes are offered in all organisational skills and processes that are regarded as important, from interviewing and appraising employees to leadership development. Job crafting, if embraced as important in the organisation, needs to sit alongside the other enabling programmes offered by L&D. Its presence in the L&D catalogue further signals its importance and implies permission to engage in it.

HR can generate buy-in by sharing the evidence that demonstrates the return on investment that job crafting creates (see *The impact of job crafting* in the box below). They can also teach the relevant skills and techniques so that all employees understand how to make it work for them and their colleagues. The buzz/drain model, job crafting concept and the re-design exercise (see the Appendix) can all be incorporated into the programmes. Clearly, high-quality L&D programmes on job crafting can be designed and implemented with relative ease and to good effect.

> ### The Impact of Job Crafting
>
> Investigations into the value of job crafting interventions have demonstrated their value. Meta-analysis revealed that, on average, workshops result in an increase in performance over three months of 14% or more. The effect is almost entirely due to the impact on employee engagement (Oprea et al., 2019).
>
> Statistics like this are helpful in conveying the value of job crafting to the leadership team and managers when gaining buy-in. However, company-specific statistics are more powerful when seeking sustained support and investment.

3. *Team Workshops*

Job Crafting can be undertaken successfully by individuals but even better when it is done as a team (Carucci & Shappell, 2020). Often, tasks deemed draining by one are a buzz for another, and in such cases, some easy realignment may be undertaken through the process of 'task swapping'. If some tasks are considered a drain to all, the team may decide to take a different approach to them. They might automate them, share them out evenly, create an incentive bonus to take them on and so on. Think back to the 'crap cart' in Chap. 7. Creativity in the team may be able to change the allocation of the work and experience of the members. Importantly, managers who fear that job crafting will create conflict or destroy productivity can bring these concerns into the open for discussion in a facilitated environment.

4. *Appraisal*

Appraisal is a rearward examination of effectiveness in any role. It tends also to be accompanied by a forward look at career development aspirations. Job crafting needs to feature in both. Any changes that have been made through job crafting in any performance year may be reviewed. Similarly, any discussion of how performance might be improved should consider job crafting as one of the possible interventions. Aspirations calling for a job crafting review and discussion can be identified. In this way, job crafting becomes a regular part of the performance landscape and enters the vocabulary of everyday employment.

5. *Strengths Discovery*

Giving employees the time and space to discover and appreciate their strengths is crucial since one of the tenets of job crafting is to personalise our roles to play to our strengths.

Strengths can be defined as *'a combination of talents (naturally recurring patterns of thoughts, feeling and behaviour), knowledge (facts and lessons learned), and skills (the steps of an activity)'* (Buckingham & Clifton, 2001*)*. Similarly, strengths are *'understood to be natural capacities that we* *yearn to use, that enable authentic expression, and that energise us'* (Govindji & Linley, 2007). Thus it is easy to see that the opportunity to play to our strengths at work will provide some of the 'buzz' that re-energises us.

Effective job crafting depends upon people knowing themselves well enough to design the work that will work for them. Human Resources can support this self-discovery process by providing employees with strengths-based assessments to help them understand themselves better.

Despite a major increase in research into positive psychology and the benefits of utilising strengths, we find people reluctant to discuss their strengths. *Can you confidently list your own strengths? Are you aware of your team members' strengths?* Their absence in any discussion may simply be because we are too modest to share them, or they may reflect that we do not know what our strengths are.

The data provided by strengths-based assessments offers employees unbiased insights into the ways in which they can alter their jobs to make the jobs work best for them. When considering the data-saturated age in which we live, where AI and algorithms make informed suggestions to shape the social media content we are shown, the television we watch and even the food we eat, such inputs are likely to be well received, and potentially even expected.

10.3 Occupational Health

We reviewed in Chap. 3 the evidence on the harmful effects of stress. In the workplace, Occupational Health practitioners can use job crafting as a tool to promote employee well-being. When employees present to Occupational Health showing obvious signs of stress or anxiety, they frequently display anger, loss of temper or levels of irritation that alienate others. Such behaviour can lead to disciplinary proceedings but sensitivity to stress and health-related issues suggests an alternative: to discover the causes of the problems rather than simply dealing with their manifestations. Occupational Health can work with employees to establish which aspects of their role may be placing too many demands on them and use job crafting as a tool to help them re-design their role in ways which better balance their resources and demands.

There are more benign versions of this same story. Perfectionists invest inordinate amounts of time in trying to do their work to the highest possible standards. They frequently take on too much and can lose sight of the pragmatic standards that make most work possible, elevating their success criteria to levels that almost nobody could attain. Job crafting could be used to address this by considering the types of work-related situations that may trigger perfectionism in an employee and design their workload, or approach to it, in light of this. For example, perfectionists struggle with tasks which lack clearly defined expectations and standards, as their own are unrealistic, and cause them to work more than is required. Applying job crafting to this issue may mean that an employee considers either 'shedding' such tasks or re-designing them in a manner which is less triggering, such as ensuring they clearly establish expectations before agreeing to take on work.

10.4 Line Managers

Team leaders, line managers and supervisors have immediate influence over employees and their working experience. Unsurprisingly, therefore, they also play a key role in influencing employees' job crafting. So we now turn to how line managers might influence their team members positively in the context of job crafting. Note that many of the actions suggested here replicate the actions suggested earlier for the leadership team.

10.4.1 Role Modelling

One of the most powerful ways line managers can promote job crafting in their teams, as with senior leaders, is to role model the behaviours they wish to promote in others. When immediate managers share their job crafting experiences with others, they signal that employees have permission to craft. Employees will interpret the activity as positive and legitimate and be more likely to do likewise.

Modelling can also improve employees' job crafting self-efficacy. By sharing their crafting experiences, managers provide employees with the opportunity to experience job crafting vicariously through them. Research shows that vicarious experiences boost individuals' self-efficacy and their judgements about their own ability to perform the behaviour (Miraglia et al., 2017). To maximise the benefit of this role modelling, managers should share their crafting experiences, including what went well, which barriers presented themselves, and how they overcame them.

10.4.2 Crafting Conversations

Managers can have conversations with employees which encourage and enable job crafting. These can be added into one-to-one agendas, become part of wider developmental sessions or even be given their own focus.

The key role of managers in these conversations is to encourage employees and provide opportunities for reflection (regarding which aspects of their job they could change) and space for exploration of how employees could act on this and choreograph their roles. Managers can also provide employees with highly valuable insights into their strengths, values and passions, made evident when working with them. We suggest starting such conversations by confirming that employees understand the concept of job crafting and the benefits of doing it (see Chap. 7), and then switching the focus to exploring future crafting objectives and plans. These are coaching conversations.

1. *Job Crafting Questions*

There are three rather different kinds of job crafting to discuss during crafting conversations: task, cognitive and relational. To explore each of these we suggest using this set of exploratory questions. They are not a script or a checklist, simply a series of possible prompts to stimulate crafting conversations.

Task: making changes to the number, type, or nature of tasks that make up work

- To what extent does your work utilise your skills?
- What is your favourite task/activity at work? Why?

- What aspects of your role do you look forward to doing? Why?
- What are you doing when you feel most skilled at work?
- If you could stop doing one of your key tasks/activities tomorrow, what would it be? Why?
- What have other people told you that you are good at?
- What work are you doing when you lose track of time?

Cognitive: reframing how we think about work in ways which build meaning and purpose

- What do you consider is the purpose of your work?
- How proud are you of the work you do? Which aspects specifically? Why?
- How does your work impact others, especially our clients?
- What motivates you to do your work?
- What are your core values? How compatible are they with your work?

Relational: modifying networks of relationships at work in terms of the number, type and intensity of interactions

- Who are you closest to at work? Why?
- Which individuals do you most look forward to interacting with? Why?
- Are there any new relationships that you would like to develop through your work?
- Is there anyone at work who you avoid or find draining? Why?

The beauty of job crafting is that there are endless possibilities and the way in which each individual chooses to craft will be different. In our experience, the magnitude of opportunities can also seem daunting to employees. So we suggest reviewing one aspect of job crafting at a time.

1. *Re-design Exercise*

   This exercise brings the buzz/drain and job crafting concepts together to provide a framework in which to conduct a role audit, reflection and re-design. It is a practical and guided way to help employees and teams consider how work can be shaped and designed in ways which better reflect them.

First, the exercise prompts consideration of the most common and important elements of an employees' working life. This involves an audit of tasks (e.g., delivering training, answering emails), relationships (e.g., with peers, managers) and cognitions (what provides a sense of meaning and purpose, e.g., recognition, financial gain and the like). These elements are then mapped onto Fig. 10.1[1] below in terms of how much they give or take energy, and how much time is invested in them. Following this, a series of questions and prompts encourage changes in the manner illustrated by the arrows in the diagram. Specifically, those which increase time spent on elements which give energy, and reducing time spent on those which drain it.

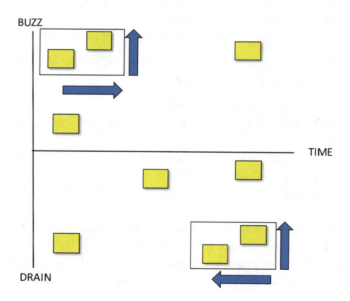

Fig. 10.1 Mapping buzzes and drains

---

[1] Compiled by the authors.

10.4.3 Crafting Experiments

Employees' responses to the crafting questions and re-design exercise can be used by managers to inform the design of crafting experiments (the actions taken in pursuit of a job crafting goal). These do not need to be wholesale job re-designs and we suggest pursuing individual ideas one by one, evaluating their success afterwards. Indeed, job crafting changes tend not to be large-scale. A CIPD study found that more than 74% of the job crafting examples they examined took employees less than 12 minutes a day (Baker & Slemp, 2018).

Experiments may have a rough and ready feel at the start and need to be refined over time or even abandoned. Once goals are established, the following prompts may help employees consider the practical ways in which they could job craft in each of the three domains:

Task Crafting

- Adding new tasks that they find exciting and engaging. Volunteer to contribute to projects relating to their interests. If they cannot utilise their strengths in their role, seek other teams and projects that could benefit from their input.
- Maximising investment into existing tasks which they look forward to and find energising. Find ways to devote more time and energy to these. Commit 30 minutes a week to practising an energising skill. Offer to teach others their favourite skills.
- Rethinking how existing tasks are conducted to make them more interesting and engaging. This can be as simple as making spreadsheets more visually appealing or conducting sleep-inducing meetings standing up or in a new location.
- Reducing and reassigning tasks that they find draining and disengaging. Use tech to automate and simplify repetitive processes. Negotiate to swap tasks with colleagues that may enjoy them more.

Cognitive Crafting

- Establish what the purpose and meaning of their work is and for whom. Write down who their work impacts and in what way; consider this in terms of both their overall role and specific tasks. Think about why the work, the organisation and industry are significant and important; what wider goals are they contributing to? Think like the cleaner at NASA who understood how he played a role in 'sending a man to the moon' and the hospital cleaners who said they 'create safe spaces for people to heal'. This reframing is powerful.
- Build their values into their work. Do more of the work that most strongly relates to their personal values, for example offering professional skills to charities relating to causes they are invested in and support. Join or form a working group related to their passions, and so on.

Relational Crafting

- Create new relationships that will serve them. Connect with a colleague with shared interests. Approach the person in the job they want to have, invite them for lunch, ask for their advice.
- Strengthen existing relationships. Create opportunities to interact more with colleagues or stakeholders that they find interesting; explore their strengths and find opportunities to collaborate, pick up the phone rather than send an email, connect with them on LinkedIn.
- Create space between themselves and those who drain them. Establish boundaries with clients and colleagues who take up unwarranted time and energy. Turn off email, Slack and Teams to allow deep work.

The following questions help to consolidate the design and also evaluate their job crafting experiments:

1. In prospect:

    (a) What strength, value or interest would I like to incorporate into my work (tasks, relationships or cognitions)?
    (b) How do I plan to do that?

(c) Do I foresee any barriers to achieving this?
(d) How do I plan to overcome these?
(e) If this goes to plan, what will that look like? What am I trying to achieve?

2. In retrospect

   (a) What happened? Was I able to job craft?
   (b) Did I experience any barriers? How did I approach them?
   (c) How do I feel now?
   (d) Would I like to maintain this?
   (e) Are there ways it could be amended to suit me better?

To reiterate an earlier caution, when having these conversations with employees, managers should exercise their awareness of the work of the team, individuals' crafting goals and experiments and individuals' attributes (strengths, interests and values) to create balance across the team. For example:

- Are there opportunities to offer task swaps? For example, other employees who have expressed interest in removing certain tasks that might engage another.
- Is the workload fairly and evenly distributed across the team? Are there any individuals who are unreasonably shedding and delegating tasks which may result in others becoming overloaded?
- Are there common tasks which many seek to remove/swap with others? Could you explore automating these, amending the way they are achieved or reframing their purpose to garner interest?

These conversations are by far the most effective when the *ideas* largely originate from the employees themselves as job crafting is essentially an employee-initiated process. It is also beneficial to ensure employees *guide* this process themselves as it builds individual investment as illustrated by 'the IKEA effect'.

10.4.4 The IKEA Effect

Anyone who has experienced a disproportionately strong sense of attachment towards even a wonky piece of furniture they have built will understand the sentiment described by 'the IKEA effect'. Described by researchers from Harvard Business School, Duke University and the University of California, the IKEA effect is a psychological bias that kicks in when we interact with objects we have made. The research found that individuals value objects which they have assembled significantly more (up to twice as much!) than identical objects which have been assembled by others.

> *Labor alone can be sufficient to induce greater liking for the fruits of one's labor: Even constructing a standardized bureau, an arduous, solitary task, can lead people to overvalue their (often poorly constructed) creations.* (Mochon et al., 2012)

People value what they create. Managers should remain conscious of this when conducting crafting conversations and avoid presenting ready-made objectives and plans for employees. Instead, be curious, encourage employees to experiment and input as much as possible. The more input and effort put into the objectives and plans by the employee, the more personally invested they will be in the output. No matter how wonky it is, it will be theirs. This is a sound coaching principle.

In addition, we know that involvement leads to commitment and follow-through. This is the compliance effect known to physicians (Pendleton et al., 2003). Studies have also shown that, when people use objects they have personalised, their performance is better than if they use non-personalised objects (Kaiser et al., 2017). Thus, by applying these principles to work and conversations about the work, and by allowing employees to personalise their roles, we will not only increase how much they value their roles but also foster improved performance.

10.5 Working with Teams

Job crafting is both an individual and a collective pursuit. Team job crafting has three steps, according to Ron Carucci and Jarrod Shappell writing in the March 2020 Harvard Business Review. The steps they describe are:

1. Identify the strategic contributions the team makes to the organisation
2. Define the aspirations and capabilities of the team
3. Distribute work across the blend of passions, skills and career aspirations of team members while ensuring the requirements of the broader organisation are fulfilled.

The clear aim is to triangulate team obligations to the organisation, the aspirations and drives of the team members and the desire for equity amongst the members. The puzzle to be solved is how to accomplish all three aims, not just one or two. This will require the collective creativity of the team. The process can also be aided by a facilitator and may additionally require the contribution of an HR business partner to ensure the conclusions reached are, or can be adapted to be, within the organisation's compensation guidelines.

Team crafting in this way requires sensitivity and mutual reciprocity between colleagues. Teammates have a collective responsibility to establish the most efficient and satisfying way of achieving their shared objectives. Doing so will require trade-offs and negotiations informed by members' individual differences. To achieve that, they need to be aware of what makes their colleagues unique; specifically, what are their strengths, interests and personal values? This practice works best once individual crafting conversations have already commenced. Coming to the session with hypothesised experiments and goals is also helpful, but not a prerequisite.

The process is relatively straightforward to outline but may need skilful facilitation to achieve. Having first reminded everyone of the shared team vision and the outcomes or goals which they need to achieve, colleagues discuss the main tasks and relationships they engage with to achieve their work. Once this is mapped out, individuals take it in turn to discuss what they see as their strengths, interests and values and their reactions to the work before inviting input and feedback from colleagues. Significantly, it is often our colleagues who recognise strengths we may not have considered before and who can inject a note of realism when they consider us to be over-reaching.

The group then works together to assign the various tasks to the best person. Elements of work can be swapped and reallocated, so individuals are doing the work they both want to and are best placed to do. The same work is being done but not necessarily by the same person or in the same way it was done before.

10.5.1 Workloads and Repetition

We know that individuals with certain personalities are more likely to job craft. Specifically, those who are more proactive and assertive. This will be reflected in teams, and there will be some who take to the practice like a duck to water and others who are more hesitant. Over time, this may result in inequities in workloads whereby crafters are shedding undesirable tasks and leaving others with too much to do. Research shows us that these behaviours cause within-group conflict and can damage team relationships (Dierdorff & Jensen, 2017; Tims et al., 2014).

Remaining mindful of others' values and drivers is helpful and the team crafting exercise needs to be revisited regularly. Conclusions reached may optimise the work and team contributions at a point in time but the situation will naturally evolve, change and surprise. The aim is to refresh and renew the insights gained and commitments forged. Psychological safety has to be maintained, irritations need to be nipped in the bud and resentments prevented. Team job crafting is analogous to keeping fit: it requires constant effort and attention but the effect is usually worth it.

This will be a continuous process of experimentation and evaluation supported by open communication. Team members should be encouraged regularly to share their experience of work and their strengths, interests and values as some will naturally shift and change over time, as we discussed in Chap. 4. People will outgrow aspirations and the challenges they will want to pursue will shift accordingly. They need to keep checking in with one another to enable teams to collectively leverage individuals' unique attributes to reach their goals.

10.6 Summary and Conclusion

When seeking to cultivate the conditions for crafting, it must be remembered that job crafting cannot and should not be enforced on anyone. By nature, it is a proactive, employee-driven process. The suggestions above are guidelines which can be used to cultivate crafting behaviours in those who wish to do so, but not to force them.

We need to approach the design of environments which enable job crafting in the same way in which we approach job crafting, experimentally and iteratively. There is no blueprint for the dynamics and differences that exist in individuals, teams and organisations, and in turn, there is no 'one size fits all' approach to making this work.

During the pandemic, we witnessed the extraordinary flexibility demonstrated by colleagues in exploring and creating new ways of working. Necessity again proved to be the mother of invention. Now we can pursue more flexible ways of working individually and collectively in the pursuit of happier and more satisfying experiences of work.

References

Baker, R., & Slemp, G. (2018). An introduction to micro job crafting: How job crafting for 12 minutes or less a day contributes to sustainable positive behaviour change. *CIPD Applied Research Conference*.

Buckingham, M., & Clifton, D. O. (2001). *Now, discover your strengths*. Free Press.

Carucci, R., & Shappell, J. (2020, March). How to job craft as a team. *Harvard Business Review*.

Dierdorff, E. C., & Jensen, J. M. (2017). Crafting in context: Exploring when job crafting is dysfunctional for performance effectiveness. *Journal of Applied Psychology, 103*, 463–477.

Edmondson, A. (2018). *The fearless organisation: Creating psychological safety in the workplace for learning, innovation and growth*. Wiley.

Govindji, R., & Linley, P. A. (2007). Strengths use, self-concordance and well-being: Implications for strengths coaching and coaching psychologists. *International Coaching Psychology Review, 2*(2), 143–153.

Hodgkinson, C. (2018). An investigation into the job characteristics and employees perceived opportunities to job craft [Unpublished Master's thesis]. University of Leicester.

Jesuthasan, R., & Boudreau, J. (2021). *Work without jobs*. MIT Press.

Kaiser, U., Schreier, M., & Janiszewski, C. (2017). The self-expressive customization of a product can improve performance. *Journal of Marketing Research, 54*(5), 816–831.

Miraglia, M., Cenciotti, R., Alessandri, G., & Borgogni, L. (2017). Translating self-efficacy in job performance over time: The role of job crafting. *Human Performance, 30*, 254–271.

Mochon, D., Norton, M. I., & Ariely, D. (2012). Bolstering and restoring feelings of competence via the IKEA effect. *International Journal of Research in Marketing, 29*(4), 363–369.

Oprea, B. T., Barzin, L., Vîrgă, D., Iliescu, D., & Rusu, A. (2019). Effectiveness of job crafting interventions: A meta-analysis and utility analysis. *European Journal of Work and Organizational Psychology, 28*(6), 723–741.

Pendleton, D., Schofield, T., Tate, P., & Havelock, P. (2003). *The new consultation. Developing doctor–patient communication*. Oxford University Press.

Roczniewska, M., Rogala, A., Puchalska-Kaminska, M., Cieślak, R., & Retowski, S. (2020). I believe I can craft! introducing Job Crafting Self-Efficacy Scale (JCSES). *PloS One, 15*(8), e0237250.

Tims, M., Bakker, A., & Derks, D. (2014). Daily job crafting and the self-efficacy-performance relationship. Journal of Managerial Psychology, 29, 490–507.

Van Wingerden, J., Derks, D., Bakker, A. B., & Dorenbosch, L. (2013). Job crafting in het speciaal onderwijs: Een kwalitatieve analyse. *Gedrag & Organisatie, 26*, 85–103.

Van Wingerden, J., Van Der Stoep, J., & Poell, R. F. (2018). Meaningful work and work engagement: The mediating role of perceived opportunity to craft and job crafting behavior. *International Journal of Human Resource Studies, 8*(2), 1–15.

11

Balance at Home

The traditional approach to achieving work-life balance has typically been to seek more time away from work in order to spend more time at home. In earlier chapters we have challenged this idea on two grounds. First, we have suggested, time at work is an important part of our lives so the very idea is flawed. Second, time at home may bring no respite from work unless the home is itself in good shape and is able to provide rest, relaxation, support and the like. But more importantly, both work and home are likely to contain a mix of support and challenge, joy and sorrow, satisfaction and frustration.

In the context of work, we have proposed that there are activities that drain our energy and others that re-energise us. The same is true at home. Home is seldom an unequivocal source of joy: it is more complex than that. Those who care for elderly and infirm relatives at home experience sadness and frustration in the midst of expressing love. There are numerous additional examples: poor quality accommodation, financial difficulties, unhappy marriages, loneliness and the like are all hard. In comparison, work may be the respite.

Yet the same argument we have applied to work can be deployed here. It is unrealistic to imagine that home is always or inevitably a balm for

© The Author(s), under exclusive license to Springer Nature Switzerland AG 2021
D. Pendleton et al., *Work-Life Matters*, https://doi.org/10.1007/978-3-030-77768-5_11

weary and aching souls. But it is entirely realistic to imagine that home can be fashioned into a good place for all those who live there. The way this can be addressed is directly analogous to the way we have described job crafting in the workplace. It starts with a realistic appraisal of the various elements encountered at home. To what extent do these energise us or deplete us? And how far can we, our fellow family members and friends, go to fashion new elements, change their frequency and intensity and create a home that achieves a significant positive balance?

Now, it may seem strange, or even inappropriate, to think of applying techniques developed for colleagues in the workplace to issues concerning family in the home. Homes, ideally, are built on loving relationships but quickly practical routines are established. Who pays the bills, does the cleaning and the shopping? What do we eat? Who are our friends? Which political party do we support? Are we religious? The answers to these and a host of other questions determine the routines in our homes and can be the source of loving sharing and caring or of domination, insensitivity and resentment.

Both at work and in the home, there are activities and relationships that can energise or drain us. Although this book is not essentially about relationships, it includes the issue in both major domains of our lives: work and home. We have the opportunity to create a range and balance of activities both at work and at home that suit us better. But we cannot achieve a sustainable life at work or at home unless we achieve a balance that also works for our colleagues and families. To do this means involving them in the creation, maintenance, analysis and change processes. In this chapter we suggest how this might be done at home, echoing these themes at work, since the steps are the same.

11.1 Why We Should Craft the Home Domain

We have discussed how job crafting can be used to make work more fulfilling and engaging by proactively managing and influencing the working experience. We have considered the importance of this, especially given that people spend a third of their adult lives at work. However, when proposing a 'new balance' for individuals, it would be naive to focus solely on the work portion of peoples' lives.

11.1.1 Personal Development

Imagine you are out socialising and are introduced to someone; they ask you about you. Would you have more to tell them about yourself in the work domain or the home domain? Which would you mention first? Either is fine, but if the current balance does not feel right to you, then this chapter will help you to consider this matter in depth.

Across our lives, we will spend a considerable amount of time planning our professional development and future careers. We set goals and aspirations, have developmental conversations, align ourselves with relevant stakeholders and engage in training and development activities. In contrast, the amount of effort, energy and time spent doing the same for our personal lives and development, which accounts for a greater proportion of our time, is often minimal. In applying the crafting methodology to the home domain, individuals can design a life outside of work which is also better aligned with their strengths, interests and values. As seen at work, these crafting efforts will bring individuals greater engagement, satisfaction and personal alignment and are likely to enhance the experience at home also.

Time spent at home is important not only for the individual but also for the organisation. The quality of life at home directly affects work because the boundaries between the two domains are increasingly permeable. The work and home domains do not exist in isolation, each influences and interacts with the other. For example, consider the frequency and intensity with which events and emotions from our home lives can spill over and affect our time at work, and vice versa. This is something of which those who lived through the coronavirus pandemic are all too aware. It saw the domains of home and work converge, and for many, become one. In creating a better life at home, work is likely to benefit.

11.1.2 Managing Resources and Demands at Home and at Work

We know that high levels of demand at work become stressors over time which can deplete individuals, detrimentally impacting their health and resulting in outcomes such as exhaustion and burnout. Often, this impact does not stop at the individual; it also extends to organisations, increasing rates of absenteeism and disengagement. However, we also know that employees experiencing high levels of job demands can take action to help them manage resources and demands to create a balance nearing equilibrium or even move to the positive. In reaching a positive balance, employee engagement and well-being are promoted. We have previously described how job crafting can be used to do this, conceptualised in this book through 'buzzes' (resources) and 'drains' (demands). Here we explain how to repurpose the same proven crafting approach to home so that a positive balance may be found there also.

One of the ways in which crafting can be used to promote a better balance is in recovery from the stresses and strains of work (Sonnentag & Kruel, 2006). Non-work recovery can include relaxation, psychologically detaching from work and learning and building new skills. While we reject the idea that work will inevitably be a demanding and draining experience and promote the use of job crafting at work, we also promote the use of crafting to build energy at home. Efforts to build resources in the home or at work impact experiences and behaviours in the other domain. Bringing skills learned at work into the home may seem obvious enough, but skills learned at home in the context of house maintenance, gardening, exercise, childcare, cookery or hobbies may prove a boon if introduced at work. The aim is to build and transfer resources in a positive cycle which ultimately results in net resource acquisition and increased engagement across both life domains. In short, making us happier.

11.2 Using Job Crafting Outside of Work

With the aim of applying the same framework and tools used for job crafting to our lives at home, there follows a series of exercises to try. The first exercise we propose focuses on tasks and relationships. Subsequent exercises will cover how we think about our lives, how we put our strengths to work and the hobbies we choose.

1. *Re-design Exercise*

The re-design exercise outlined in Chap. 10 can also be utilised to inform how we can shape and design our future leisure time. This process is thorough so we have described it in detail in the Appendix.

2. *Home Crafting Questions*

In addition to the re-design exercise, the following questions and prompts have been designed to create additional space for reflection and to fuel your considerations regarding how your future leisure time could look and how you could achieve it.

Tasks

- During your downtime, are you engaging in activities that suit your strengths, values and interests?
- If not, could you change the scope or type of activities that you already do to make them better suited to your strengths, values and interests?
- Are there new activities that you could take up that would better suit your strengths, values and interests?
- Are there any activities or skills you might enjoy but have not taken up for fear of not being 'good enough' or it being 'too late' in life to pick it up?
- Are there any activities that might suit better your current stage in life?

- Are there any childhood interests or passions that you wish you had not given up? Could you pick them back up? If not, why not?

> Do not be afraid to be ambitious. We have a friend who, at 50, decided to embark on her A-levels. She then did a degree and finally a PhD which she finished at 63, and all purely for her own enjoyment and fulfilment. Now, she has just finished writing a book based on her PhD which will soon be published.

Relationships

- Think about the people you spend time with outside of work. Of those, who do you look forward to spending time with? Who have you seen in the past and left feeling happier and more energised than when you arrived? Why? How could you spend more time with them?
- Are there any people who you dread seeing, regularly cancel plans with or feel drained after spending time with? Why? Is there a way to minimise the extent to which they drain you by seeing them in a different setting, by doing different things with them, or just by seeing them less often?
- Who do you count as your closest friends? Have you seen them enough recently?
- Of the people you choose to spend time with, who aligns with your values and who does not? Does any difference in values bring benefits (e.g. enjoying debating with a friend) or not (e.g. makes the friendship seem inauthentic/ misaligned)? Would you like to see them more or less often?

Cognitions

'Cognitive crafting' relates to changing how we think about our lives, especially in terms of the meaning and purpose that we take from it. It sounds clichéd, but to address your home time in this way, you need to find your 'why': your purpose and pay attention to your sense of 'self'.

The insights from the re-design exercise can be used to inform this process. We suggest considering some of the following:

- Does using the tips to review similarities within and differences between your buzzes and drains highlight where you may find more meaning and purpose in your life?
  - For example, if most of your buzzes related to caregiving, volunteering and spending time with family and friends, what does this suggest for the meaning and purpose around which you are building your life?
- What do you do outside of work that makes you happiest? Why?
- What gives you a sense of accomplishment? Why?
- What makes you excited? Why?
- What do you do outside of work that you are most proud of? Why?
- What meaning do you take from what you do outside of work? Why?
- How does what you do outside of work benefit you? Why?
- Who benefits from what you do? Why?
- Do you think that the things that you do outside of work are aligned with your personal values? Why?

Asking 'why?' after each prompt is designed to challenge you to think deeper. The prompts are encouraging you to question why you do what you do, to understand better the meaning and value you associate with it, how this relates to you as an individual and why your life is significant and meaningful. It echoes some of the issues to do with the 'self' we raised in Chap. 4.

If this exercise reveals ways in which your life could be made more fulfilling or meaningful through the addition/alteration/removal of tasks and relationships, or by reframing how you think about life, then we would encourage you to use the questioning and action planning framework in the re-design exercise to ensure the steps are taken to implement these changes.

3. Strengths Utilisation

Strengths and how they can be applied to the work domain have been discussed in previous chapters. The application can be extended into the home domain and our lives beyond the workplace.

Our strengths are our unique skills, talents and capabilities, and we optimise our ability to perform and function at our best when we play to them, when we engage in activities which are congruent and complementary. Ensuring that we understand our strengths places us in good stead to design our leisure time to utilise them. Playing to our strengths also energises us.

It may be beneficial to revisit your strengths as they, or the way in which they are framed, may differ slightly when thinking about them in the context of home. To do so, we propose these following steps:

- *Review your list of strengths* in the work domain and think about how they apply to the context of home. Include the skills and knowledge that you have developed across all your life experiences.
- *Consult others*. You may be very modest and reluctant to define your strengths. It can be helpful to talk to others and ask them for honest feedback regarding what they think your strengths are. Engage with your partner, parents, children, friends and colleagues.
- *Revisit previous feedback*. Think back to times when people have thanked you for something you have done, told you about how you have made a difference in their lives or complimented you on your skill or knowledge.
- *Take a test*. There are many online strengths of questionnaires you can complete for free. For example, have a look at the VIA Survey of Character Strengths which can be accessed at: https://www.viacharacter.org/.

To start establishing opportunities to apply strengths to the home domain, we suggest cross-referencing findings from the re-design exercise with your list of personal strengths. For example, someone could identify that activities relating to interacting with, supporting and helping others improve their fitness gives them a 'buzz'. In addition, they could also have strengths relating to being highly organised and methodical. Such an individual might want to combine the two to offer project management or administrative services for a gym or sports club that helps and supports others. Doing so would enable them to engage in an activity which gives them energy and plays to their strengths.

As we move through our lives with our family and friends, it is easy to see them as we did when we first met them and not stay in touch with how they, and we, are changing: the skills we are mastering and the knowledge we are acquiring. In this way we are at risk of growing apart unwittingly. Staying in touch with how our partners, other family members and we ourselves are changing and developing can keep relationships strong and current. Taking a strengths-based approach can help us to live more effectively together alongside one another at home.

4. *Hobbies*

Hobbies stimulate, energise and absorb us. They typically represent highly personal choices and are, in the literal sense, amateur activities: carried out for the sheer love of them. They provide opportunities to socialise with like-minded individuals, provide challenge, teach patience, develop skills, improve knowledge, boost confidence and self-esteem, and reduce boredom. They may also bring us face to face with success and failure.

Hobbies may be further opportunities to play to our strengths, indulge in our interests and extend the activities we enjoy at work, or they may offer a total change. We have known a professional engineer and power station general manager who, as a hobby, ran the village model steam train club, doing more of what he loved, maintaining and driving the train at weekends for the children of the village. Another aerospace engineer and project manager whose hobby was reading and writing Persian poetry: a complete contrast. Hobbies can indulge us but also extend and develop us. As an adjunct to work, they can provide further opportunities for stimulation and that paradoxical entity: relaxation through activity rather than rest. They help us express the complete person we are.

Nobody has to have a hobby, but given their benefits and the increasing amounts of time all of us are likely to have, either at work through more automation or at least in retirement, it may be a good idea to consider the following questions:

- Did you have any prior hobbies that you wish you had not stopped doing?
- Do you have any hobbies currently? What are they?
  - What it is about them that you enjoy?
  - Which parts would you drop if you could?
- Are there any skills or forms of knowledge that you wish to develop?
- What are you interested in but get little time to engage in?
- What do you wish you could do more of at work that might become a hobby at home?
- If you long for a complete contrast from what you do at work, what might that be?

11.3 Summary and Conclusion

We all spend a great deal of time outside of work, whether or not we are in employment. Home is not the antidote to work: both work and home are important parts of our lives and can be refreshed in similar ways. We can find a balance in each place between those activities that deplete us and that refresh and renew us. The same crafting techniques that help us analyse and change our work can also serve us at home and can be similarly shared with those we love as with those who are our colleagues.

A complete and happy life is likely to require a measure of balance. This is not 'work-life balance' as most people think about it but balance at work and balance at home.

Appendix: A Re-design Exercise

Here is an exercise which brings the buzz/drain and job crafting concepts together; it will help you to re-design your life and can be conducted in terms of life at work or at home. Before completing, we recommend reading the book and reflecting on the prompts, questions and exercises throughout as these will inform your responses. We also suggest that the exercise is conducted focusing on either work or home, alone. Following this, should you wish to take a holistic view of the two and 'life craft', insights can be combined to seek further opportunities by considering meta-themes, synergies and interplays between the two domains.

Re-design Exercise

1. *Audit*

First, we will conduct an audit of your life; understanding and acknowledging where we are now is the starting point which then informs where we want to be and how we plan to get there.

Take a set of post-it notes and write down the key and most important elements of your life in the context of the three domains: tasks,

Table A1 Examples

Domain	Tasks	Relationships	Cognitions
Where does this happen?	*What do you do?*	*Who do you interact with?*	*In what do you find purpose/meaning? (Your 'WHY')*
Work	Delivering training	Peers	Recognition
	Answering emails	Manager	Competition
	Team meetings	Clients	Money
	Checking reports	Peer—Jane	Development
	Coaching	Supplier—Ben	Innovation
Home	Cooking	Partner	Helping others
	Reading	Children	Family
	Gardening	Siblings	Learning
	Walking	Drama group	Social connection
	Working	Friend—Lucy	Adventure

Compiled by the authors

relationships and cognitions. N.B. Stick to one per note as the next step requires these to be moved around. *Examples* might include (Table A1):

One of the home examples relates to work. This is deliberate as the elements noted down should provide an accurate representation of how your time is spent and what is important to you. In reality, many do conduct work during their time at home. Whether this is out of choice, and to be maintained, or out of necessity and to be designed-out, is to be addressed in the following steps.

2. *Map*

Then, consider the following two questions to map each of the elements onto the diagram displayed on Fig. A1:

1. How much does this element 'drain' me and deplete my energy versus how much does it give me energy and a 'buzz'?
2. Relative to the other elements, how much time do I spend on this?

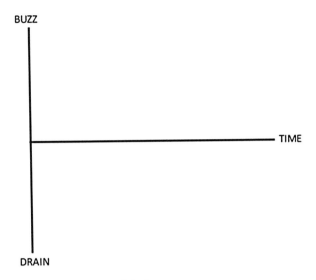

Fig. A1 Mapping the buzzes and drains

- For example, how much time do I spend on that task, with that individual, or doing things which play to this area of meaning and purpose

> Try creating your own diagram on a large piece of paper, a whiteboard or even a wall. Using string, different pens/highlighters and stickers can make the process more visual and engaging. If you prefer to capture information digitally, try the Lucidchart website.

3. *Reflect*

Once populated, reflect on the distribution of the elements of your life. Consider:

- Overall, are there more buzzes or drains? Is this a surprise?
- How is most of your time spent? On elements which give or drain energy?
- What is your initial reaction to this? Does this balance feel right? How do you feel? Satisfied, disappointed, excited, disheartened?

- Are there any elements which you are immediately drawn to change (e.g., would you like to remove elements or add new ones, increase or reduce the time spent on any elements)? Note these down for later.

If the answer to the last question suggests you benefit from making a change or two, consider the following prompts to identify opportunities to make small, but significant changes like those illustrated by the arrows in the diagram (Fig. A2 as compiled by the authors).

4. Re-design

Look at the bottom right-hand corner of the diagram where the outlined box is in the example. These are the elements that you find draining and spend a lot of time engaging with. These are likely to have a disproportionately negative impact on your overall levels of happiness and satisfaction with your life.

Of the group of elements in this area, choose one which you would like to change. Consider where you would prefer it to be on the diagram

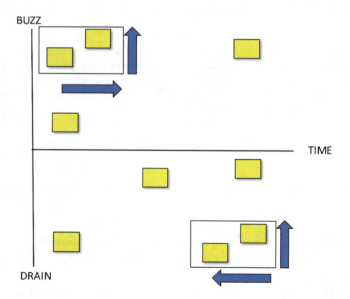

Fig. A2 Mapping the buzzes, drains and possibilities

and try answering the following questions that have been designed to help you think of the ways in which you could move it. Capture any ideas you have as you go.

- *To reduce the amount of time I spend on this 'drain', I could…*

> This could include making processes more efficient, time limiting or automating the task—think *'work smarter, not harder'*! After all, what are robot vacuum cleaners and Excel formulae for?
>
> Consider 'shedding' the activity. Could you find a way to stop doing this? Could you find a way to delegate it to someone else, negotiate with a partner or colleague to swap it in return for taking on responsibility for a different and less draining activity? This might be a case of *'I'll cook, you clear up'* or *'I'll do the VAT return if you write this piece of thought leadership'*.

- *What is it about this element that makes it 'drain' me? Why?*

> Review the group of elements in the 'drain' area of the diagram. Do these have any commonalities? For example, do they play counter to your strengths, relate to something in conflict with your personal values, relate to something you do not find interesting or take place with individuals or groups you find disengaging? Looking for themes such as these may help to identify why these activities 'drain' you. You might love volunteering but struggle to connect with those who you do it with, or your investment in a working group may be dwindling because your opinions have since changed.

- *To make this less of a drain or more of a buzz, I could:*

> Focus on the aspects of the element that make it draining. Is it the activity itself, who you do it with, where you do it, how frequently you do it? Seek to change that aspect, this will not always be the element itself, it is often its design. For example, a weekly pub quiz with friends may be something you have come to dread, but changing your attendance to monthly, or even swapping teams, may make it a buzz again.

Look at the elements in the outlined box at the top left-hand side of the diagram. These are the elements that give you energy, but on which you currently spend little time. They present real opportunities to boost your levels of happiness and satisfaction with your life.

Identify one element in this area which you would like to focus on changing and use the following prompts to brainstorm ways in which you could do that.

- *To spend more time on this 'buzz' I could:*

> Think about ways in which you can create more opportunities to engage in this element, or others which give you a similar 'buzz'. If it relates to an interest, consider joining a club or setting aside more protected time to do it alone.
>
> Could you share the aspect of this element which gives you a buzz with others to generate more chances for you to do it? For example, if it related to a personal passion such as tennis or data analysis, invite someone to join you at a tennis match or at a conference, offer to teach them and share your expertise.

- *What is it about this element that makes it give me a 'buzz'? Why?*

> Review the group of elements in the 'buzz' area of the diagram. Do these activities have any common features? For example, do they have a shared purpose, do they play to your strengths, relate to interactions with similar people or groups, or do they occur in similar settings? Looking for themes such as these may help to identify why these activities give you a 'buzz'.

- *Are there any other elements that I could amend or introduce that would give me a similar 'buzz'? To do so, I could…*

> Seek out opportunities to play to what gives you a 'buzz'.
>
> For example, if you notice that tennis gives you a buzz because it offers opportunities to compete with others, you may wish to increase your time spent engaging in this by signing up to tournaments or even taking up another sport.
>
> If getting to know others is what gives you a buzz, look at other elements that relate to people. If you also enjoy reading or teaching, could you consider writing about someone you have known? In this way, a psychologist friend has started investing her paternal grandfather with a view to writing his biography.

Table A2 This is what I am going to do

Table Appendix.2 This is what I am going to do				
What:	**Who:**	**When:**	**Date completed**
Action steps I need to take	People I need to involve (for support or accountability)	I aim to achieve this by (date)	

5. *Act*

Consider the actions and ideas that you have captured working through the exercise and choose *two* to commit to doing, soon! Committing to small, well-defined and achievable goals maximises the likelihood of success (Table A2).

Collective Crafting

The re-design exercise is very personal and focused on the individual. In addition, insights from the activity can be used for collective benefit. For those who share their home and working environments with others, try getting them involved in the exercise. To do so, we suggest completing the activity as individuals first, then talking through the findings with each other in addition to highlighting any actions that you have committed to doing.

As those we work alongside and share our homes with are likely to know us well, they can provide their own insights and reflections!

Try asking one another:

- Whether there are any other prominent elements which could be added to the initial audit.
- Their opinions regarding the mappings of the various elements? Does it appear accurate?

- If they see any themes regarding what gives you a buzz or drains you.
- If there are other ways in which you could maximise enjoyment from, and time spent on, elements which give you a 'buzz'.
- If there are other ways in which you could minimise the amount of energy 'drains' take or reduce the time spent on them.
- Could you 'swap' any elements that one finds draining and the other finds more of a buzz?

For example. Parents could swap aspects of childcare duties, or colleagues could swap client relationships, so that they attend to the responsibilities most aligned with their own strengths, values and interests.

Index[1]

A

Absenteeism, 32, 149, 168
Adapt, 50, 53, 54, 60, 62, 73, 106, 145
Age thirty transition, 45
Aging population, 63
Algorithms, 152
Alienation, 62
Amateur, 81, 82, 173
Ambiguity, 91, 127, 130
Ambitions, 1, 85
Amygdala, 94
Anti-discrimination, 63
Appraisal, 151
Artificial intelligence, 126
Aspirations, 45, 64, 140, 151, 161, 162, 167
Augmented reality, 126
Automate, 62, 119, 136, 151, 157
Automation, 58
Autonomy, 17, 26, 28, 32, 33, 35, 118–120, 123, 145, 147

B

Baby Boomers, 34
Balance, vii, ix, 2–4, 7–20, 27–29, 35, 36, 44, 49, 59, 75–87, 91–93, 98, 100, 105, 118, 126, 141, 148, 152, 159, 165–168, 174, 177
Bennet, Tony, 83
Breakthrough, 67, 71
Brexit, 68
British Airways, viii, 86
Burnout, 30, 32, 33, 118, 168
Buzz/Drain, 78–80

---

[1] Note: Page numbers followed by 'n' refer to notes.

© The Author(s), under exclusive license to Springer Nature Switzerland AG 2021
D. Pendleton et al., *Work-Life Matters*, https://doi.org/10.1007/978-3-030-77768-5

Index

C

Career development, 151
Carnegie, Andrew, 10, 11
Catastrophe, 58
CATCH-30s, 50
Cognitive crafting, 115–116, 158, 170
Collective crafting, 181–182
Complementary differences, 128
Complexity, 32, 91, 127, 130
Compliance, 15, 16, 20, 34, 82, 132, 160
Computerisation, 61
Computers, 58
Condensed work weeks, 149
Convergence, 126, 131
Coronavirus, 2, 20, 65, 127, 133, 134, 149, 167
Crafting conversations, 154–157
Crafting experiments, 157–159
Creativity, 25, 33, 36, 49, 129, 136, 161
Culture, 32, 42, 63, 107, 120, 128, 130–132, 135, 136, 138–140, 143, 145, 148, 149
Customised working, 149
Cygnus, 134

D

Danaher, 139, 140
Deadline Decade, 50
The delighted, 78, 79
Demand-control-support model, 30
Demands, 7, 16, 28, 30, 32, 78, 118–120, 123, 129, 138, 144, 147, 152, 168
The depressed, 78, 79
Developmental tasks, 51
Displacement of workers, 126

Disruption, 45, 50, 59, 60, 66–71, 126, 127
Distributed working, 65
Driverless car, 59
Drudge, 61, 84, 85, 91, 98

E

ECT, 87
Eddington, Rod, 86
Einstein, 57
Elements or our work, 89
Employee-initiated, 109, 143, 159
Employee life cycle, 119
Employee resource groups, 114
Employeeship, 107–109
Employment, 1, 3, 4, 8–10, 12, 15, 16, 18, 21, 22, 24–26, 34, 60, 62–64, 77, 120, 149, 151, 174
Empowerment, 8, 109, 143
Energy, vii, 3, 21, 25, 27, 32, 33, 36, 48, 52, 76, 78, 79, 82, 84, 91, 118, 120, 132, 133, 141, 147, 156–158, 165, 167, 168, 173, 176, 177, 179, 182
Engagement, 20, 30, 33, 63, 105, 109, 117, 138, 149, 150, 167, 168
Exercise, 95–97
The exhausted, 76, 79
Exhaustion, 32, 33, 168
Externalising, 94, 99

F

Factories, 25, 64
Farms, 60, 62
Feedback, ix, 86, 101, 118, 146, 162, 172
Flexibility, 28, 62, 91, 147, 148, 163

Flexible working, 148
Forceful features, 91
Forces, 3, 15, 57, 62, 65–71, 81
Forecasters, 57
4IR, 126, 127
Freelancing, 63
Frequency, 62, 91–93, 99, 100, 166, 167
The frustrated, 77, 79
The future of work, 57–73

G
Gardeners, 140
General Practitioner, 90, 101, 102
Generations, 34–36, 44, 59, 63
Generation Ys, 34
Generation Z, 34
Genome editing, 126
Gig, 63
The 'gig' economy, 63

H
Happiness, 50, 78, 105, 115–117, 133, 178, 180
Harvard, 33, 83, 140, 160, 161
Health and Safety Executive, 31
Henley, ix, 4n1, 83, 84
Hobby, 78, 80–83, 173, 174
Home crafting, 169
Homelife, 79
Human-centred, 126
Human-machine collaboration, 61
Human-machine competition, 61
Human resources, 17

I
ICA, 84
Identity, 21–26, 44
IKEA effect, 159, 160
Impact, 21–23, 28, 29, 32, 52, 64, 68, 70, 71, 87, 89, 91–94, 98, 100, 103, 115, 116, 118, 120, 121, 126, 133, 148–150, 155, 168, 178
Individuation, 41
Industrialisation, 10, 62, 64, 125
Industrialised countries, 119
Industrial revolution, 10, 15, 17, 59, 125, 126
Intensity, 25, 91, 155, 166, 167
Interests, 11, 17, 45, 101, 103, 109, 112–114, 116, 117, 119, 122, 138, 147, 157–159, 161, 162, 167, 169, 170, 173, 182

J
JCSE, 144
Job crafting, 3–4, 53, 89, 105–111, 115–120, 122, 123, 127, 130–132, 135–137, 141, 143–163, 166, 168–175
Job crafting self-efficacy, 144
Job descriptions, 106, 145, 149
Job design, 106–108, 121
Job redesign, 106
Job satisfaction, 44, 109, 117

L
Leadership, vii, 4, 16, 32, 62, 63, 67, 68, 72, 90, 102, 107, 108, 125, 127, 128, 130–140, 143, 146–150, 153

Index

Leadership tasks, 131–140
  building and sustaining relationships, 135
  creating alignment, 132
  delivering results, 137
  leading, 137, 138
  planning and organising, 133
  setting strategic direction, 131
  team working, 136
Legacy concepts, 61
Leisure, 7, 36, 81, 126, 129, 169, 172
Life craft, 175
Life phases, 42, 54
Life stages, 39, 53, 101
Life structure, 44–47, 49–51, 53
Line managers, 4, 147, 153
Lockdown, 25, 65, 149
Luddite, 59

M

Machine metaphor, 17–18
Manufacturing, 60, 125
Meaning, 16, 20, 23–25, 30, 33, 36, 44, 47, 48, 63, 86, 115, 119, 121, 122, 155, 156, 158, 170, 171, 176, 177
Megatrend, 132
Mental health, 21–23, 25, 31, 47, 136
Menzies, John, 139
Meta-analysis, 150
Mid-life crisis, 85
Mid-life transition, 45–47
Millennials, 34, 35
Morale, 25, 32, 86, 93, 113, 149

N

Net score, 92, 93
Neuroplasticity, 28
Neuroscience, 26, 94
9/11, 86
Novice Phase, 43–44

O

Occupational Health, 4, 147, 152–153
OECD, 2, 8, 59
Oxford, ix, 61, 81, 83, 84

P

Pandemic, 2, 4, 20, 25, 41, 65, 68, 69, 72, 77, 86, 127, 130, 133, 134, 149, 163, 167
Passages, 47–50
Perceived opportunities, 144
Perfectionists, 153
Performance, 26, 27, 29, 31, 106, 117, 150, 151, 160
Person-job-fit, 109
Philanthropy, 10–12
Positive affect, 117
Positive, negative or neutral, 91
Positive psychology, 152
Prediction, 66, 126
Primary Colours Approach to Leadership, 4, 128
Productivity, 30–32, 40, 60, 72, 151
Propositions, 128
Psychological benefits, 26
Psychological safety, 145
Purpose, 16, 18, 20, 23, 25, 26, 29, 36, 44, 50, 52, 53, 63, 70, 86,

Index

90, 106, 112, 115, 119, 121, 122, 126, 128, 132, 138, 140, 155, 156, 158, 159, 170, 171, 176, 177

Q
Quality of life, 65, 167

R
Radiologists, 64
Reactive or proactive, 100–103
Recessions, 2, 20, 148
Reinventing, 129, 138
Relational crafting, 113–114, 119, 158
Remote working, 2, 149
Resilience, 109, 136
Retirement, 24, 50, 69, 83, 102, 119–120, 173
Robotics, 126
Rockefeller, John D, 10
Role clarity, 147
Role descriptions, 106
Role model, 153
Rowntree, Joseph, 10–12

S
Salutogenesis, 29–31
Scaling, 91
Scenarios, 57, 65–73, 75–79, 134
Schwab, Klaus, 126
S curves, 51–52
The seasons of a man's life, 42–47
Self-actualisation, 28
Self-sustaining, 3, 84, 140, 141

Service industries, 60, 65
Shedding, 153
Slavery, 8, 9, 18
Social intelligence, 61
Social support, 22, 23, 30, 114, 118
SPACES, 26
Spinning jenny, 59
Star Trek, 57
Strengths-based assessments, 152
Stress, 26–29, 34
Supermarket manager, 90, 92, 93
Supervisors, 153
Sustainable employment, 120
Systems, 58, 59, 65, 125, 138, 139, 149

T
Task crafting, 111–113, 119, 157
Task swapping, 112, 151
Team crafting, 161
Technology, 2, 4, 16, 35, 46, 54, 58–61, 65, 67, 68, 70–72, 114, 126, 140
Terra Incognita, 60, 126n1
3-D printing, 126
Thriving, 109
TIDES
   demographic changes, 69
   environment and Ethics, 69–70
   institutional change, 68
   shifting social values, 70–71
   technology, 59, 60, 64, 67–68, 73
Time travel, 57
Tipping point, 35, 60, 72
Top-down, 106–107, 143, 145
Trade union movement, 15–17
Transitions, 3, 39–54, 85, 119
Trying Twenties, 49
Turnover, 31, 32, 149

U

Uncertainty, 48, 50, 57, 127, 130
Unemployment, 2, 22–24, 60, 76
University lecturer, 90, 98
Unpredictability, 127, 130, 133

V

Values, 2, 11, 12, 18, 20, 23, 34, 35, 39, 44, 63, 70, 109, 112, 114, 116, 117, 119, 122, 130, 132, 134, 135, 138, 154, 155, 158, 159, 161, 162, 167, 169–171, 182
Videoconferencing, 25, 65
Virtual, 2, 18, 65, 114
Vision, x, 12, 24, 61, 63, 87, 129, 131, 132, 138, 161
Volunteering, 83, 114, 171
VUCA, 127, 130

W

Welfare State, 15
Wellbeing, 29, 30, 105, 117–119, 148, 152, 168
WHO, 28, 69
Women, 13, 14, 22, 23, 31, 40, 42n1, 62
Workforce, 3, 4, 9, 15, 16, 34, 35, 58–60, 62–65, 73, 107, 115, 123, 129, 149
Working from home, 86
Work-life, ix, 2, 3, 7–20, 34, 75–87, 141, 165, 174
Workload, 29, 32, 33, 118, 153, 159
Workplace, 3, 25, 30, 33–36, 43, 44, 58, 64–65, 73, 76, 82, 85, 106, 108, 119, 129, 130, 133, 137, 141, 146, 147, 149, 152, 166, 172
World Economic Forum, 59, 126

Z

Zara, 64

Printed in the United States
by Baker & Taylor Publisher Services